Minority Rights

D0916476

KEY CONCEPTS

Published

Barbara Adam, *Time*
Alan Aldridge, *Consumption*
Alan Aldridge, *The Market*
Colin Barnes and Geof Mercer, *Disability*
Darin Barney, *The Network Society*
Mildred Blaxter, *Health*
Harry Brighouse, *Justice*
Steve Bruce, *Fundamentalism*
Margaret Canovan, *The People*
Anthony Elliott, *Concepts of the Self*
Steve Fenton, *Ethnicity*
Michael Freeman, *Human Rights*
Fred Inglis, *Culture*
Jennifer Jackson Preece, Minority Rights
Paul Kelly, *Liberalism*
Anne Mette Kjær, *Governance*
Ruth Lister, *Poverty*
Michael Saward, *Democracy*
John Scott, *Power*
Anthony D. Smith, *Nationalism*

Forthcoming

Darin Barney, *The Network Society*
Harriet Bradley, *Gender*
Craig Calhoun, *Community*
Atejandro Colás, *Empire*
Keith Dowding, *Rational Choice*
Tim Dunne, *International Society*
Katrin Flikschuh, *Freedom*
John P. S. Gearson, *Terrorism*
James Gow, *War*
Russell Hardin, *Trust*
Robert H. Jackson, *Sovereignty*
Bob Jessop, *The State*
Peter jones, *Toleration*
Keith Krause and Michael C. Williams, *Security*
Chandran Kukathas, *Multiculturalism*
Jon Madel, *Global Justice*
Anthony Payne and Nicola Phillips, *Development*
Judith Philips, *Care*
Chris Phillipson, *Ageing*
Raymond Plant and Selina Siong-Li Chen, *Citizenship*
Kenneth Prandy, *Social Mobility*
Jennifer Jackson Preece, *Minority Rights*
Stuart White, *Equality*

Minority Rights

Between Diversity and Community

Jennifer Jackson Preece

polity

Copyright © Jennifer Jackson Preece 2005

The right of Jennifer Jackson Preece to be identified as Author of this Work has been asserted in accordance with the UK Copyright, Designs and Patents Act 1988.

First published in 2005 by Polity Press

Polity Press
65 Bridge Street
Cambridge CB2 1UR, UK

Polity Press
350 Main Street
Malden, MA 02148, USA

ISBN: 0-7456-2395-6
ISBN: 0-7456-2396-4 (pb)

A catalogue record for this book is available from the British Library.

Typeset in 10.5 on 12 pt Sabon
by Servis Filmsetting Ltd, Manchester
Printed and bound in Great Britain by MPG Books Ltd, Bodmin, Cornwall

The publisher has used its best endeavours to ensure that the URLs for external websites referred to in this book are correct and active at the time of going to press. However, the publisher has no responsibility for the websites and can make no guarantee that a site will remain live or that the content is or will remain appropriate.

Every effort has been made to trace all copyright holders, but if any have been inadvertently overlooked the publishers will be pleased to include any necessary credits in any subsequent reprint or edition.

For further information on Polity, visit our website: www.polity.co.uk

Contents

For Farfar and Djeda

Preface

I have been involved in researching and teaching minority rights and related issues in Canada and the United Kingdom for more than a decade. So when I was approached by Polity to write a short book on this topic for their Key Concepts in the Social Sciences series, I naively thought this would be a relatively quick and easy way to capitalize on my previous experience. But as I began to think more deeply about the underlying logic of minority rights, I realized that this assignment was more challenging, and interesting, than I had originally anticipated. After considerable reflection, I came to the conclusion that the key concepts and assumptions behind minority rights can only be fully understood as one response to a much deeper 'problem of minorities'. That problem is not confined to the era of nation-states but may arise in any historical period. 'Minorities' are political outsiders who challenge the prevailing principle of legitimacy. This explains why the identity of those persons who constitute a 'minority' changes from one political and historical context to another. And it immediately discloses how minority questions enter into both domestic and international politics – for what defines legitimacy within a community also has a fundamental effect on relations between communities. The perspective I have adopted in this book is normative without being prescriptive; it is fundamentally concerned with changing ideas of what constitutes 'right conduct' towards minorities as disclosed in law and policy at both the domestic and international level. For at its core, the 'problem of minorities' is what Isaiah Berlin has termed a 'collision of values' between diversity and community to which there can be no permanent resolution (Berlin 1990: 13). The best minority rights can do is provide us with a moral and legal framework in which hard choices can be adjudicated. But at the end of the day we are nevertheless doomed to choose between the interests of the minority and the political community in whose territory it resides.

In writing this book I have incurred debts to institutions and individuals whom I wish to acknowledge. Some of my early attempts to elucidate the 'problem of minorities' were made at the Failed States and Global Governance Conference in 2000 and 2001, the Cambridge/Dartmouth sponsored project on the Future of Human Rights in 2000 and 2001, the Carnegie Council founded project on Complex Power-Sharing in Post-Conflict Divided Societies in 2002 and 2003, the University of Glasgow's Department of Politics Seminar Series in 2002, the British International Studies Association Conference in 2002, the University of Glasgow's Law Department Roundtable on Self-Determination and International Law in 2003, the International Studies Association Conference in 2003 and the Humboldt University Roundtable on Minority Rights and Education in 2004. I would like to express my appreciation to all who were involved in these conferences for their comments and suggestions on these papers.

I would also like to thank friends and colleagues who in various ways, either directly or indirectly, helped me reach closure on this project. Some provided dialogue, criticism and encouragement as the work proceeded while others influenced or provoked my thinking by their own work on similar topics: Chaloka Beyani, Richard Bronk, Chris Brown, Jack Donnelly, Kevin Featherstone, Antonio Figuiera, Montserrat Guibernau, Bob Hancké, John Hutchinson, Abby Innes, Corinne Lennox, Margot Light, Gene Lyons, James Mayall, Anja Mihr, Cornelia Navari, Brendan O'Leary, Anthony Ristic, Tome Sandevski, Gwen Sasse, Waltraud Schelkle, Anthony Smith, Georg Sørensen, Michael Stohl, Paul Taylor, William Wallace, Marc Weller and Nick Wheeler. I am also grateful to the anonymous readers of Polity, who generously provided a careful and constructive criticism of my argument which was invaluable in making the final revisions.

My greatest intellectual debts are owed to Will Bain, Emma Haddad and Robert Jackson, each of whom engaged me in constant conversation on these and other themes throughout the writing of this book. Their sharp wit and incisive comments have had an enormous influence on my thinking and no doubt improved the quality of my argument. Finally, this study could not have been written without the love and support of my husband, Steve Preece, my parents, Robert and Margaret Jackson, and my ever-faithful companions Pekoe (the cat), Poacher (the labrador) and Paddy (the cocker spaniel). Any errors of fact or judgement which remain are entirely my own.

What sparks a particular academic interest, and many an academic career, is often deeply personal. That is certainly true in my case. I have dedicated this book to the memory of my two grandfathers – Johannes Jokumsen (born in Sundby in Lolland, Denmark in 1895), who became John Jackson, and Josip Prpic (born in Lovinac in Lika, Croatia in 1903), who became Joe Perpick. It was their immigrant experience in the United States and Canada during the early part of the last century that first drew my attention to minority questions.

Abbreviations

ACHR	American Convention on Human Rights
CEDAW	Committee on the Elimination of all Forms of Discrimination against Women
CERD	Convention on the Elimination of all Forms of Racial Discrimination
COE	Council of Europe
CSCE	Conference on Security and Cooperation in Europe
DEDR	Declaration on the Elimination of All Forms of Intolerance and of Discrimination Based on Religion or Belief
ECHR	European Convention on Human Rights
EU	European Union
ICCPR	International Covenant on Civil and Political Rights
ICTY	International Criminal Tribunal for former Yugoslavia
ILO	International Labour Organization
MOST	Management of Social Transformations Programme
NATO	North Atlantic Treaty Organization
OSCE	Organization for Security and Cooperation in Europe
UDHR	Universal Declaration of Human Rights
UNCHR	United Nations Commission on Human Rights
UNESCO	United Nations Educational, Scientific and Cultural Organization

1
Understanding the 'Problem of Minorities'

Introduction

On 22 April 1993, a young man called Stephen Lawrence was brutally murdered while waiting at a London bus stop. Stephen Lawrence was on his way home with a friend when they arrived at the bus stop at around ten-thirty that night. Stephen was approached by a group of five or six youths. The group quickly and literally engulfed him. During this time one or more of the group stabbed Stephen twice. The group of murderers then disappeared. The whole incident probably lasted no more than 15 or 20 seconds (Stephen Lawrence Inquiry 1999: 1.1–1.10).

By any standards, this was an awful and tragic event. Yet the public interest it generated far exceeded what would ordinarily be expected from an attack of this kind. Since 1993, Stephen Lawrence's murder has been the subject of thousands of newspaper articles and television programmes, a civil court action and ultimately a public inquiry into his death. What set Stephen Lawrence's murder apart was not the violence of the crime, the human tragedy it represented, nor the fact that his murderers remain unpunished: the death of Stephen Lawrence and the failure to find and convict those responsible has an added significance because of the fact that race was a defining feature in this case. Stephen Lawrence was black and his murderers were white: more than that, his murder was 'simply and solely and unequivocally motivated by racism' (Stephen Lawrence Inquiry 1999: 1.11). Worse still, the subsequent police investigation was itself marred by, among other things, 'institutional racism' (Stephen Lawrence Inquiry 1999: 46.1). Stephen Lawrence belonged to a 'racial minority' and he had a right not to be attacked or discriminated against on the basis of his race. Accordingly, Stephen Lawrence's death raised larger questions about the ways in which the London Metropolitan Police and British society more generally treat persons belonging to minorities.

Two years after Stephen's death (on 7 July 1995), several thousand Bosniak men and boys were murdered in Srebrenica when what had hitherto been a UN 'safe haven' in the Yugoslav wars of secession fell to Serbian forces under the command of general Ratko Mladić (Silber and Little 1996: 345–50). Like Stephen Lawrence, these men and boys were singled out and killed because they belonged to a minority; they were victims of what has come to be known as 'ethnic cleansing'. The 'Srebrenica massacre' raised equally important questions about the role of international society in protecting persons belonging to minorities. The perceived failure to act in 1995 became a major justification for NATO bombardment of Serbia-Montenegro in 1999, ostensibly to halt 'ethnic cleansing' in Kosovo. Since this time, Ratko Mladić has been indicted for genocide, crimes against humanity and violations of the laws or customs of war by the International Criminal Tribunal for former Yugoslavia (ICTY). In 2001, Radislav Krstić, a Serb commander who led the assault on Srebrenica alongside Mladić, was convicted by the tribunal on genocide charges and received 46 years–life in prison (Drumbl 2004).

Both the murder of Stephen Lawrence in London and the 'Srebrenica massacre' in Bosnia point to a much deeper issue in contemporary social and political life which we might conveniently term 'the problem of minorities'. This book interrogates both the substance of that problem and the various public policy responses it has provoked: Why is diversity so often regarded as a threat to political community? Does stability really require homogeneity? Or can it be maintained in the presence of different minority groups? Will a minority rights response finally resolve the 'problem of minorities'? Or is a permanent solution likely to remain illusive?

The 'problem of minorities'

The 'problem of minorities' is both intellectually created and historically situated. In its current form, it is a consequence of the fundamental shift in political thinking with regard to the appropriate relationship between legitimacy and community which took place in Europe from the eighteenth century to the mid-nineteenth century and by 1945 had become the basis of a global international order. Whereas previously authority came from above (the ruler, the divine), today we believe that it originates from below (the people). But, as Ivor Jennings famously remarked, while 'on the surface it seemed reasonable: let the people decide. It was in fact ridiculous because the people cannot decide until someone decides who are the people' (Jennings 1956: 56).

How shall the people be identified? On the basis of sociological criteria such as religion, race, language or ethnicity? Or on the basis of juridical criteria such that political communities (colonies, constituent units of federations, etc.) determine the people and not the other way around? What if the people are not one but many? Which people shall rule and on what basis?

It is precisely at this point that the existence of religious, racial, linguistic and ethnic diversity – and hence minorities – within contemporary states becomes controversial. Does political order require conformity with the prevailing definition of political membership? Or can political community be maintained even in the presence of diversity? What rights, if any, should be accorded to those who are different? Are the rights of equal citizenship sufficient to ensure their individual freedom and political participation? Or should we also be concerned to preserve and promote their distinct identities? In other words, what should our response be to that 'diversity dilemma' which is a consequence of the imperfect realization of self-determination within the present states system? Questions like these are only intelligible in the context of particular normative assumptions about the ways in which political life *ought* to be organized.

Diversity which contradicts the principle that legitimates a political community is likely to be problematic regardless of whether or not the community in question is a medieval universitas (a community that recognizes no limits to its authority and aspires towards the global membership of all humankind), a dynastic state, a nation-state, a multicultural state or some other form of community yet to be imagined. A principle of legitimacy embodies current judgement about the basis for independent political community and membership within it: which communities may claim the equivalent of what we now refer to as sovereignty; how territories and peoples may be transferred or acquired; how succession is regulated when larger communities break up into smaller communities or when several communities combine into one (Wight 1977: 153). Such principles shape relations within as well as between communities and thus 'mark the region of approximation between domestic and international politics' (Wight 1977: 153) which is precisely where the 'problem of minorities' is located.

Humankind is currently politically organized into approximately two hundred sovereign, territorial states, each one embodying a separate normative tradition shaped by the vagaries of its history and its political, ethnic, religious and other traditions. Nevertheless, extensive diversity remains at the sub-state level. Practically speaking, this sub-state diversity cannot be fully or finally accommodated by the further redistribution of existing sovereignty to create more independent states. As a former United Nations Secretary General noted in 1992, 'If every ethnic, religious or linguistic group claimed statehood, there would be no limit to fragmentation, and peace, security and economic well-being would become ever more difficult to achieve' (Boutros Boutros-Ghali 1992: paragraphs 17–18).

Consequently, a potential for 'the problem of minorities' exists within most contemporary states. In 1985, Walker Connor could identify only seven homogeneous states with no border problems – Denmark, Iceland, Japan, Luxembourg, the Netherlands, Norway, and Portugal: together these account for less than four per cent of the world's population (as quoted in Moynihan 1993: 72). And even this short list is somewhat deceptive. For example, Denmark possesses a historic German minority in what was once a much contested border region. Moreover, contemporary flows of immigrants, migrants and refugees are a new source of diversity in these and other states around the globe. This is evident in Western

Europe where the long-term effects of multiethnic and multi-racial immigration have become a recent focus of political controversy and public policy. And although new states have been recognized in the period since 1985 (most notably in the territory previously belonging to the Soviet Union, Czechoslovakia and Yugoslavia), this redistribution of sovereignty has in many cases exacerbated rather than ameliorated the 'problem of minorities' (as, for example, in Croatia, Bosnia, Serbia-Montenegro, Macedonia, Russia, Moldova, Georgia and Azerbaijan). Clearly, the 'problem of minorities' may have very serious consequences not only for the individuals concerned but also for domestic, regional and indeed global peace and security. A proper understanding of the dilemmas which give rise to such conflict is thus essential for both academics and policy makers interested in minority matters.

Diversity as a dilemma

Minority questions are among the most contested issues in political life because they speak to an inherent tension in human affairs between competing desires for freedom and belonging. Since Aristotle, we humans have been identified as 'political animals' because of our predisposition towards social interaction. We do not exist as atomistic individuals abstracted from society but rather as socialized individuals embedded within a well-defined social and political order. For this reason, most contemporary political theorists, following John Rawls, assume that people are born into and lead a complete life within the same society and culture such that this context delineates the scope within which people must be free and equal (Rawls 1993: 277). Thus the desire for social belonging is an essential human characteristic and a prerequisite for that condition of peace and stability in which the human personality may flourish.

Significantly for the study of minorities, there is a fundamental paradox implicit within this characterization of the human condition. Freedom and belonging may be equally important for human flourishing but they nevertheless remain mutually incommensurate and potentially competing values. Freedom requires autonomy of action; belonging requires coordination and in some situations subordination of autonomous action to preserve the social relationship on which it is based. Freedom necessitates and indeed perpetuates a diversity of choices and so promotes a variety of values, beliefs and identities; belonging necessitates and indeed perpetuates social cohesion and so constrains choices to preserve a common identity and its concomitant values and beliefs. Freedom encourages innovation; belonging encourages orthodoxy. Freedom creates diversity; belonging creates uniformity. At some point, these values will collide and that collision is likely to foster uncertainty, suspicion, fear and even conflict. It is precisely this collision of values which makes the existence of diversity within humankind, especially that religious, racial, linguistic and ethnic diversity which has long been a hallmark of distinct human communities, a potential source of insecurity and conflict.

Most people want to associate with other people like themselves: people with whom they can feel at home. It is only to be expected that these differences should eventually give rise to a plurality of communities, and so human experience up to and including the present time reveals a diversity of social groupings including families, tribes, nations, states and civilizations. Different communities are likely to espouse different and perhaps even contradictory values as the basis of their political order. My god may not be your god. Your ways may not be my ways. And in some situations, your god or your ways may threaten the very foundation of my god and my ways. For example, the Romans could not tolerate the Jews and Christians precisely because the monotheism intrinsic to Judeo-Christian beliefs was fundamentally at odds with the cult of the emperor intrinsic to Roman beliefs. In such circumstances, diversity is incompatible with the survival of the prevailing political order; either the problem of diversity must be eliminated or the political order must be changed to accommodate it. The Romans famously persecuted the Jews and Christians in the hope of forcing them to conform with Roman religious beliefs and practices; ultimately, of course, the new Christian religion triumphed and the pagan empire of the Caesars was transformed into the Catholic empire of the popes.

The potential for controversy and even conflict arises because of the intrinsic incommensurability of belonging manifested as community and freedom manifested as diversity. This explains both the tendency towards suspicion and fear of those who are different and why such fears are often politically manipulated within highly developed political communities like states wherein social complexity is assumed to require a correspondingly increased degree of conformity. Hannah Arendt explains this tendency in her study of the origins of totalitarianism:

> Our political life rests on the assumption that we can produce equality through organization, because man can act in and change and build a common world, together with his equals and only his equals. The dark background of mere givenness, the background formed by our unchangeable and unique nature, breaks into the political scene as the alien which in its all too obvious difference reminds us of the limitations of human equality. The reason why highly developed political communities, such as the ancient city-states or the modern nation-states, so often insist on ethnic homogeneity is that they hope to eliminate as far as possible those natural and always present differences and differentiations . . . because they indicate all too clearly those spheres where men cannot act and change at will, i.e., the limitations of the human [political] artifice. The 'alien' is a frightening symbol of the fact of difference as such, of individuality as such, and indicates those realms in which man cannot change and cannot act and in which, therefore, he has a distinct tendency to destroy. (Arendt 1972: 301)

Political order is, precisely as Arendt describes it, a human artifice: it is a consequence of human conduct rather than a part of the natural, physical world around us. Political discourse and action is fundamentally moral discourse and action: it deliberately constrains freedom defined as the ability to do exactly as one pleases with reference only to one's own esoteric and idiosyncratic needs, desires, ambitions and so forth by establishing a common ethical standard. Such normative constraints on individual behaviour are the foundation of an ordered and thus secure collective existence. As Thomas Hobbes reminds us, without this human artifice which he terms 'Leviathan' there is 'no place for industry . . . no arts, no letters, no society; and which is worst of all, continual fear and danger of violent death; and the life of man, solitary, poor, nasty, brutish and short' (Hobbes 1988: 66). It is the abiding fear of a return to the natural (non-social) order (what Hobbes describes as a 'war of all against all') that makes the existence of diversity, especially that diversity which challenges the normative basis of the prevailing political community, so controversial.

Where diversity is understood to contradict, weaken or destroy collective belonging and social consensus, it becomes a subject of policies designed to ameliorate these socially and politically destructive effects. History has demonstrated time and again that once homogeneity is accepted as the ideal basis of political organization, the individual liberty of members of minority groups becomes precarious. In such circumstances, the political community tends to act as if it is single and unitary (Cobban 1970: 109). And if in practice this is not the case, it must endeavour to make the facts correspond to the ideal regardless of the rights and interests of those among its population who don't conform to the official public identity – and discrimination, assimilation, persecution, ghettoization, forced expulsion and even genocide may follow from this imperative.

The minority rights approach takes an altogether different view of diversity. It does not consider the existence of minorities to be a prima facie threat to political order. Instead, one of its central premises is that minorities who are recognized and supported by the state are less likely to challenge its authority or threaten its territorial integrity. Consequently, the proponents of minority rights seek to justify not only government toleration but also positive government action to promote diversity and to affirm the dignity, esteem and mutual respect of all citizens whatever their religious, racial, linguistic or ethnic identities. Minority provisions of various kinds are already evident in the governmental arrangements of Austria, Belgium, Canada, Denmark, Germany, India, Italy, Spain, Switzerland and the United Kingdom, to name only a few. And the clear implication of international developments in this area, both at the United Nations and in European regional organizations, is that more states should adopt such practices. Although the 1992 United Nations Declaration on the Rights of Persons Belonging to National or Ethnic, Religious and Linguistic Minorities is a non-binding agreement, the standards it endorses are nevertheless meant to be taken seriously. Accordingly, state compliance in this area is monitored by the United Nations Working Group on Minorities and the United Nations Sub-Commission on the Promotion and Protection of

Human Rights to which it reports. In Europe, the presumption in favour of minority rights is even stronger. Thus, for example, the European Union's accession criteria for prospective members as stipulated in the Copenhagen Criteria of 1993 includes 'respect for and protection of minorities'. And both the Council of Europe and the Organization for Security and Cooperation in Europe have dedicated monitoring mechanisms intended to ensure that member states give effect to their minority rights undertakings.

Minority rights aim to prevent conflict by encouraging domestic circumstances in which the religion, race, language and ethnicity of all peoples can be preserved and promoted within existing borders. Majorities are required to respect minorities' desire to preserve their way of life, while at the same time the minority is required to respect the majority's right to do the same and on this basis unilateral minority efforts to secede from the existing state are precluded. However, negotiated political settlements between groups compatible with democratic practices are encouraged – and where these opt for the creation of new states (as in the so-called 'velvet divorce' whereby Czechoslovakia was replaced by Slovakia and the Czech Republic), international society will of course respect the wishes of the parties concerned. Such minority practices thus disclose a prior consideration for both democratic principles and the territorial status quo: the principle of self-determination is set in the context of respect for existing territorial boundaries and political action is primarily directed at preventing violence within existing states rather than encouraging the recognition of new states, except where this is an outcome of bona fide democratic negotiation.

Minorities as political outsiders

No universally agreed definition of 'minority' exists at the present time precisely because the 'problem of minorities' often manifests itself in efforts to distinguish between those who belong to a political community and those who do not.

Minorities are political outsiders whose identities do not fit the criteria defining legitimacy and membership in the political community on whose territory they reside. As we shall see, in the medieval Catholic universitas, individuals with religious beliefs that did not correspond to those of the Catholic Church constituted minorities; in dynastic states, minorities were those who did not comply with the religious predilections of the sovereign prince; in European overseas empires, minorities were those who did not possess the defining characteristics of (European) 'civilization'; in nation-states, minorities were those who did not possess whatever characteristics were constitutive of the 'national identity'; and so forth.

Because the exact identity of a minority changes according to the prevailing definition of political community, the concept 'minority' is notoriously difficult to generalize. Common usage defines a minority as 'a smaller number or part, especially within a political party or structure' (*OED* 1989). The assumption here is that an inferior numeric status presupposes an inferior political status, but that is not always the case. A memorandum prepared by the UN Secretary General in 1950 highlights the inadequacy of using a definition based upon a group's demographic size within a state's population: 'The term minority cannot for practical purposes be defined simply by interpreting the word in its literal sense. If this were the case, nearly all the communities existing within the state would be styled minorities, including families, social classes, cultural groups, speakers of dialects, etc. Such a definition would be useless' (United Nations 1949: 85). Ultimately, what matters is not size but belonging: minorities are those who are denied or prevented from enjoying the full rights of membership within a political community because their religion, race, language or ethnicity differs from that of the official public identity. For example, in colonial Kenya the political community was defined by the British imperial government and the white European settlers who constituted a tiny percentage of the total population. Africans comprised the vast numerical majority but were nevertheless excluded from the body politic because they failed to satisfy the prevailing 'standard of civilization'.

Because of situations like that in colonial Kenya, minorities are often described as being 'non-dominant', that is, not in a position of control or authority within a political community. This emphasis on 'non-dominance' is an attempt to ensure that the term 'minority' is not improperly applied to 'dominant' numerical minorities such as the European population of the Kenya colony or the white population of apartheid South Africa. In other words, it excludes those groups who exercise control or authority within a political community even if in strict demographic terms such ruling communities are outnumbered.

The concept minority, as applied to religious, racial, linguistic or ethnic groups, is of relatively recent origin. It dates from the 1919 Paris Peace Conference when the term 'minority' was included in the peace treaties with the successor states of the Habsburg Empire, Ottoman Empire and Prussian Kingdom (Laponce 1960: 3). Since this time, 'minority' has come to refer mainly to a particular kind of community, and especially to a national or similar community which differs from the predominant group in the state (United Nations 1945: 85). The date 1919 is significant as the moment when Woodrow Wilson put his new principle of legitimacy – self-determination – to work in the hope of creating a more just and therefore lasting international order.

The contemporary 'problem of minorities' thus emerges as a lack of consent or entitlement to full participation in political life such that the principle of self-determination is compromised in some way. Minority status is therefore generally restricted to citizens of a state – and so excludes refugees, resident aliens or migrant workers – to underscore the significance of membership in a political community and the presumption in favour of full incorporation within it. The treatment properly accorded to refugees, aliens or migrants has in each case its own distinct normative basis and so it is argued these should be treated as separate categories (Minority Rights Group 1991: 7). The same rationale applies to questions of gender, sexual orientation and physical disability. Accordingly, separate areas of law and policy have emerged to address these issues. For example, at the United Nations, problems of discrimination against women are dealt with by a separate committee dedicated to this purpose, namely the Committee on the Elimination of Discrimination against Women (CEDAW). Minorities are in a position to claim special treatment in the form of minority rights precisely because they are not fully integrated into or do not exercise control over their own political community. They are thus 'imperfectly' or 'incompletely' self-determined.

This conclusion raises the important question of whether or not special provisions for minorities are transitional arrangements designed to integrate such groups and the persons belonging to them into the larger body politic, thereby transforming 'outsiders' into 'insiders'. For those who take a transitional view, once self-determination has been realized, then minority status can no longer be said to apply and any special arrangements deriving from such status may be reasonably terminated. This was the position of the great powers during the interwar period, when the League of Nations System of Minority Guarantees was created for the new or enlarged states of Central and Eastern Europe. As Sir Austin Chamberlain observed at that time, 'The object of the minorities treaties was to secure for the minorities that measure of protection and justice which would gradually prepare them to be merged in the national community in which they belonged' (League of Nations 1929: 51). Similar claims are put forward today by the critics of affirmative action policy directed at racial minorities, who argue that the original rationale for such measures no longer pertains.

Alternatively, it may well be that the ideal of providing special arrangements for particular groups and/or the persons belonging to them is becoming part of the way we think about and practise self-determination and democratic government. Recently, it has been suggested that new developments directed at minorities may be modifying the substance of self-determination to include internal arrangements for autonomy or self-government which fall short of separate statehood. We see evidence of such provisions in a range of recent agreements intended to ameliorate self-determination disputes between minorities and majorities: examples include the General Framework Agreement for Peace in Bosnia (the 'Dayton Agreement') (1995), the Northern Ireland Peace Agreement (1998), The Bougainville Peace Agreement (2001) and the Constitutional Framework for Provisional Self-Government in Kosovo (2001), among others.

These developments would seem to offer a new perspective on the traditional understanding of the relationship between self-determination and democracy. John Stuart Mill famously remarked in his 1861 treatise *On Representative Government* that 'free institutions are next to impossible in a country made up of different nationalities' (Mill 1972: 392–3). For more than a century, that presumption worked against the recognition of minority rights that would perpetuate distinct cleavages within the state. Now, however, the idea of democracy has itself been reconsidered, and indeed redefined, by liberals who have come to recognize the need for a social consensus which is more than just 'majoritarian'. Far from 'disappearing', it is increasingly assumed that a minority which is fully integrated into the political community will nevertheless remain identifiable as a distinct group. Moreover, minority rights may be of continuing significance for the members of such groups not only because of the cultural, economic or political advantages that they confer but also because of their symbolic value. In other words, minority rights may be emerging as a permanent attribute of political membership in democratic states.

Minority rights

The idea of special arrangements for minorities is by no means a recent innovation. Within Europe there was a historic practice of linking boundary changes with special provisions for any minorities created as a result of the territorial readjustment. We see evidence of such arrangements in virtually all of the major treaties of the seventeenth, eighteenth and nineteenth centuries. Eventually, this practice culminated in the League of Nations System of Minority Guarantees, which sought to preserve the 1919 territorial settlement in Central and Eastern Europe. When that system failed to prevent the events leading up to World War II (many of which, like the Sudeten Crisis of 1938, concerned minorities), the international protection of minorities was discredited and largely abandoned for much of the Cold War (Jackson Preece 1998b).

This older discourse on minorities was not articulated in the language of 'rights' but that of 'guarantees'. The semantics here are significant because they tell us how these arrangements were constructed. 'Minority guarantees' were state obligations either voluntarily assumed as a gesture of goodwill towards a particular group or state (usually kin-states of the minority in question) or externally imposed upon new or weak states by the great powers in the interests of international peace and stability. Such arrangements were primarily intended to preserve the territorial integrity of existing states and not to satisfy the moral claims or grievances of minorities per se. Accordingly, these 'minority guarantees' were relatively easy to repudiate when it was in the state's interest to do so (Jackson Preece 1998b: 55–66 and 85–90). Normative priority was therefore accorded to the state and, by extension, the society of states to which it belonged rather than to the minority individual or group.

Since 1945, and the emergence of the human rights discourse, special provisions for minorities have become known as 'minority rights' rather than 'minority guarantees'. The rights discourse is an almost ubiquitous feature of contemporary politics. States, international and non-governmental organizations, individuals and groups all increasingly speak the language of rights. In part, such developments are a consequence of the growing recognition of a variety of rights at both the domestic and the international level but they are also much more than that. The salience of the rights discourse and indeed the domestic and international standards it invokes is an important reminder that politics is normative as well as instrumental. International agreements, state structures, public policies and so forth entail moral issues – questions of good and bad, right and wrong (Jackson 2000: 38). To claim a right transforms what might initially be viewed as a mere expediency into a moral imperative. In other words, the power of the rights discourse originates in its normative content and corresponding moral authority. Whereas 'guarantees' exist at the discretion of the guarantor, 'rights' are normative entitlements which adhere to the rights holder. For this reason, rights are comparatively more difficult to limit, repeal, annul or abolish and thus afford the possibility of greater protection. That is why minorities and those who advocate recognition of their claims have chosen to express themselves in a new 'minority rights' discourse rather than the older language of 'minority guarantees' .

Yet, despite its widespread appeal, the idea of 'rights' is far from obvious. Instead, there is often a great deal of confusion between the use of right as an adjective (the description of right conduct) versus the use of right as a noun (something one has) (Vincent 1986: 8). 'Rights' in the latter sense are conduct that 'one may legally or morally claim' which gives rise to normative circumstances of 'being entitled to a privilege or immunity or authority to act' in a certain way (*OED* 1989). The idea of a right as a normative entitlement is the 'stock-in-trade' of lawyers and thus is usually a feature of legal (e.g., international treaties and domestic constitutions or statutes) or quasi-legal (e.g., non-binding international resolutions and documents) provisions. A right in this sense consists of five main elements:

> a right holder (the subject of the right) has a claim to some substance (the object of a right), which he or she might assert, or demand, or enjoy, or enforce (exercising a right), against some individual or group (the bearer of the correlative duty), citing in support of his or her claim some particular ground (the justification of a right). (Vincent 1986: 8)

For example, as an individual (the right holder) I may claim a right to property (the object of the right) which I assert in the form of ownership and exclusive enjoyment (the exercise of the right) against other potential property holders, be these individuals, companies or indeed the state (the bearers of the correlative duty), on the grounds that I should be able to enjoy the proceeds of my own labour (the justification of the right).

Rights may be held either by individuals or by groups. Individual rights are designed to preserve and protect the autonomy of persons as individuals. Group rights are designed to preserve and protect the individual's propensity for communal attachments and associations. Individual rights are held by individuals either as humans or as members of specific groups (for example, citizens of a particular state or members of minority communities). Group rights are held by corporate entities. In international law, the classic group rights are the right of sovereignty held by states and the right of self-determination held by peoples. There is currently a great deal of discussion in both academic and policy-making circles about the relative merits of individual versus collective formulations, particularly as these would apply to sub-state groups and their members (Lyons and Mayall 2003). Nevertheless, for the most part, current practice recognizes only individual rights which adhere to persons belonging to minorities and not the rights of minority groups themselves. Instead, a collective element is preserved indirectly through the proviso that such rights may be exercised either individually or in community with other members of the group.

Are 'minority rights' simply a subset of 'human rights'? Or are such arrangements best thought of as an entirely separate normative category? There is considerable controversy on this point within the 'rights' literature. 'Human rights' are commonly classified into civil and political, economic and social, or cultural rights according to the substance of their provisions (Donnelly 2003; Sieghart 1986; Vincent 1986). In this formulation, 'cultural rights' include all rights directed at the preservation of and participation in cultural communities. Since minorities frequently wish to preserve and promote their cultural distinctiveness, 'minority rights' are sometimes viewed as synonyms for 'cultural rights'. Critics, however, point out that such a characterization not only fails to recognize the political and economic claims of minorities (for example, to special representation in governmental bodies or autonomy within their historic territories or an appropriate share of public revenues necessary to fund minority schools and so forth) but may in fact legitimize and thus perpetuate the very 'majoritarian' policies and institutions that minorities themselves regard as 'unjust' or 'oppressive' (Kymlicka 1995; 2001). Here, too, the dispute over semantics points to a deeper dilemma: 'minority rights' do not come as a given. Those who agree in principle that minorities should be accorded rights of some kind may nevertheless disagree, sometimes passionately, about what substantive provisions these ought to include. Thus, as we shall see, the debate is not merely over whether minorities should have rights, but also what those rights should be.

Conclusion

The aim of this book is to locate current legal and policy debates on minority rights in a larger context of evolving norms and practices dealing with the 'problem of minorities'. Careful attention will be paid to the ways in which different constructions of community (including religious universitae, dynastic states, civic nation-states, ethnic nation-states, European overseas empires, multicultural states and international society) shape and define the 'problem of minorities' and the various solutions which have been put forward to overcome it. Each chapter will provide a historical overview of a particular minority identity – religion, race, language and ethnicity – and how it came to assume a social and political significance in the present and recent past that it may not have possessed in the more distant past. In so doing, attention will be paid to both domestic and international laws and policies relevant to the minority in question and how developments in one area often influence those in the other. The last part of each chapter will provide a summary of the rights currently ascribed to that minority and highlight the main controversies which surround these provisions. In this way, I hope to demonstrate that 'minorities' and 'minority rights' are not natural givens but the constructions of particular historical moments. By way of conclusion, the final chapter will reflect upon the hard choices which are likely to arise even when one adopts a minority rights response to the 'problem of minorities'.

The organizational structure employed here corresponds with those identities currently included in the 1992 United Nations Declaration on the Rights of Persons Belonging to National or Ethnic, Religious and Linguistic Minorities, the 1966 International Convention on the Elimination of All Forms of Racial Discrimination, and article 27 of the 1966 International Covenant on Civil and Political Rights, which together comprise the current global standard on minority rights. Other actors such as states and regional organizations may improve upon this standard, but they cannot go beneath it without risking international sanction. Because national identity may be defined by religion, race, language and ethnicity – or indeed some combination thereof – the minority issues relating to it are not addressed in a separate chapter but instead appear in recurring sub-sections throughout the book. However, the argument has been deliberately ordered so as to make it possible for readers particularly interested in national identity questions to read these sub-sections consecutively and thus obtain a comprehensive coverage of minority practice in that area.

2
Religion

Introduction

Religion may be defined as 'recognition on the part of man of some higher unseen power as having control of his destiny, and as being entitled to obedience, reverence, and worship' (*OED* 1989). It involves not only the 'general mental and moral attitude resulting from this belief, with reference to its effect upon the individual or the community' but also 'personal or general acceptance of this feeling as a standard of spiritual and practical life' (*OED* 1989). In other words, religion has two dimensions: the one private and deeply personal arising out of the innermost convictions of the individual; the other public and resulting from the practical effect of those convictions not only on the individual but also on the community to whom he or she belongs.

While religious belief may be best described as an internal state of mind, the exercise of that belief is to a large extent a social practice sustained by shared doctrines, myths, rituals, sentiments and institutions. Rites of religious worship tend to be collective rather than individual and are generally performed for the benefit of a community of believers. In other words, it is usually through a community that the practice of religion is conducted and perpetuated. Consequently, religion implies more than a relationship with the divine – it also involves human relations between both believers and non-believers.

Religion is not simply about what we believe but also about how we conduct our lives. Accordingly, religion may determine what we eat, how we dress, the language we speak, how we raise our children, the days we work, whether or not we carry arms or are prepared to support or engage in violence, what secular laws we will obey and which we will resist and so on. This social dimension of religion explains why religious values, myths and symbols can readily acquire a broader cultural significance such that religion often helps shape and define ethnic, national or civilizational identities. It is this social dimension which makes religion a potential diversity dilemma.

Religion as a diversity dilemma

Religion is among the oldest sources of collective identity and belonging. Archaeological evidence suggests that religion has played a central role in the organization and legitimacy of human communities throughout history and across cultures – this is true of the ancient Hebrews, Egyptians, Persians, Tibetans, Mayans and Aztecs, among others (Wuthnow 1998: 733–5). At the same time – and for just as long – religion has also been a key factor distinguishing human communities and a potential source of tension between them. As early as the sixth century BC, we find evidence of warfare motivated by religious convictions: at this time, Cyrus the Great of Persia set out to conquer the Mediterranean world because he believed that this would hasten the end of time as prophesied by Zoroaster (*Encyclopaedia Britannica* 2005b).

Religion continues to play an important part in contemporary life. Many of the myths and symbols which underpin existing ethnic and national identities have their origin in older religious associations and practices (Smith 1986). Around the globe, whether in Northern Ireland, former Yugoslavia, Lebanon, Israel/Palestine, Tibet or Nigeria, to name only a few examples, religious differences are a source of controversy and discord. Some commentators have gone so far as to suggest that global politics itself is increasingly characterized by a 'clash of civilizations' which has its origins in divergent religious traditions (Huntington 1997).

It is undoubtedly the case that religion remains an integral part of the lives of millions of men and women in every region of the world; that is so regardless of whether or not they belong to a majority or to a minority. Why? Because as the European Court of Human Rights has observed, 'religion is one of the most vital elements that go to make up the identity of believers and their conception of life' (Evans 1997: 283). In other words, religion matters to both individuals and their communities, which is precisely why it can give rise to difficult diversity dilemmas.

Religion becomes a diversity dilemma in those circumstances where religious beliefs and the practices they necessitate conflict with the authority of the political community and the values which underscore it. Dilemmas like these have a long history in human relations. One early version of just such a conflict is immortalized in the Christian Gospel when Jesus Christ is asked whether Jews should pay Roman taxes. Noting that a denarius (Roman coin) is inscribed with Caesar's image, Jesus replies, 'Render therefore unto Caesar the things which be Caesar's, and unto God the things which be God's' (Luke 20: 25).

Unfortunately, this solution to the problem – to separate religious duty from political obligation – is not always easily attainable. So, for example, while the Roman Empire was able to accommodate the religious beliefs of many of its subject peoples provided that these peoples in turn recognized the divinity of Roman gods – and in particular the Roman Emperor or Caesar – this practice foundered when it confronted the monotheistic beliefs of the Jewish and later Christian minorities. In a monotheistic belief system like Judaism and Christianity there can be only one god and thus it was not possible for the Jews or the Christians to incorporate Roman deities into their religious practices without breaking their own religious codes. If one recognized the divinity of Caesar, one ceased to be a Jew or a Christian. Unfortunately, however, the authority of the Roman Emperor was based upon his supposed divinity – hence for the Romans the refusal to recognize the divinity of the emperor was perceived as a 'challenge to the secular authorities and a threat to civil order' (Evans 1997: 19). In other words, 'Christianity could not be fitted within the framework of the [Roman] Empire and, ultimately, one would have to yield' to the other (Evans 1997: 18). There followed a long series of Roman persecutions directed at the early Christian community until Christianity itself became the official religion of the Roman Empire in AD 380. It is precisely in situations like those pertaining in the Roman Empire between the first and the fourth centuries AD, where religious beliefs preclude political obligations or vice versa, that religion becomes a potent diversity dilemma.

Religion within community

Religion has political significance precisely because it exerts such a powerful influence over the values, identities and human conduct of those who believe in it.

This makes religion both a potential basis for and indeed rival of political community. Broadly speaking, therefore, the relationship between religion and political community may take one of two forms: political community may be imagined as coextensive with religious membership, thus precluding the acceptance of religious diversity; or alternatively, political community may be imagined as distinct from religious membership, thus opening up the possibility for the acceptance of religious diversity. Where political community is considered coextensive with religious community, religious minorities are likely to be viewed with suspicion or even hostility and their position is usually precarious. At best, religious minorities may be tolerated and at worst they could find themselves subject to policies of discrimination or persecution. In contrast, where political community is imagined as distinct from religious community it is more likely that religious minorities will be accepted within the body politic.

Toleration is fundamentally different from acceptance: to tolerate is 'to endure or to forbear' that to which we are otherwise ill disposed, whereas to accept is to 'regard favourably or treat as welcome' (*OED* 1989). Toleration is a negative policy of restraint, whereas acceptance is a positive policy of support. In circumstances of toleration, religious homogeneity remains the preferred option but is considered impracticable due to prevailing social, political or economic conditions. As a result, some at least of the religious minorities within a political community are given limited freedom to worship according to their distinct beliefs and customs. Specific religious minorities may be deemed to have reasonably close affinities with the dominant religious beliefs and practices of the political community and on this basis acquire a preferential position. Alternatively, particular religious minorities may perform useful social or economic functions and, in exchange for these services, receive a limited amount of protection from the political authorities. Or it may well be that guarantees for religious minorities are necessary in order to maintain peaceful relations with neighbouring communities of their co-religionists. In all of these cases, religious toleration will extend only so far as is necessary for political order and stability. Thus the interests of the political community will unavoidably trump those of the religious minority when the two come into conflict.

In circumstances of acceptance, religious diversity is positively welcomed. Yet even in the most hospitable of political conditions, hard public policy choices between competing values (e.g., religious symbols versus public symbols, the sanctity of religious buildings versus public security, etc.) are nevertheless likely to arise. Thus the reasonable limits of religious freedom, especially as this applies to minorities, are likely to remain a potential source of controversy even within political communities which accept religious diversity.

Religion and medieval universitas

The rival Catholic and Islamic universitae of the medieval period provide telling examples of what happens to religious minorities when the political community is at one and the same time also a religious community. As heirs to the Judaic tradition, Christians and Muslims share the belief that God rules the world by delegating important functions to a special people (Bozeman 1960: 233).

This prophetic monotheism underscores a vision of community as a universitas which ultimately seeks to unite the whole of humanity in the worship of the 'one true God'. From this perspective, faith rather than blood, language or jurisdiction is the primary social bond: for the devout, one is a Christian or a Muslim first and a German, Italian, Turk or Egyptian second. Accordingly, where theological dogma acquires the force of law and religious principles provide the foundation for political life – as in the medieval Christian and Islamic universitae – the general assumption is that territories should be homogeneous in religion, i.e., all Christian or all Muslim (Bozeman 1960: 235).

During the medieval period, Western Europe was united in a single universitas which existed to serve and defend the Latin Christian rite. At this time, the only real state in the modern sense was the Catholic Church (Figgis 1922: 15). The pope's *plenitudo potestatis* was the medieval equivalent of the modern idea of sovereignty. The ultimate source of authority both secular and religious was the Christian god. The pope was his representative on earth and ruled the world in the name of Jesus Christ. On this basis, the pope could remove the mandate of secular kings and princes, including even the Holy Roman Emperor. Moreover, the authority of the pope was territorially unlimited. In principle, if not in practice, it extended across the entire globe (Wight 1977: 130). Christianity thus became the raison d'être of every aspect of medieval European life.

The only salient differences between members and non-members in medieval Catholic Christendom were those premised on religion. Consequently, a complex vocabulary arose which distinguished 'apostasy', or the total rejection of Christianity by a previously baptized Christian, from 'heresy', or the rejection of one or more orthodox Christian doctrines by someone who maintains a general belief in Jesus Christ and his teachings. It also discriminated (albeit less clearly in actual usage) 'pagans', or those who practise idolatrous rites and profess polytheism, from 'infidels', or those who belong to rival monotheistic religions (notably Judaism and Islam) (*Catholic Encyclopedia* 1908).

An equally well-developed lexicon of religious difference may also be found in the medieval history of Islamic norms and practices. In this context, Muslims were distinguished from 'People of the Book' or *kitabis* (non-Muslims who believe in the heavenly revealed scriptures, e g., Christians and Jews), and the 'People of the Book' or *kitabis* were in turn distinguished from 'Unbelievers' or *nasaara'hs* (van der Vyver and Witte 1996: XXXIII). The millet system, which prevailed in the Ottoman Empire from the fifteenth century to the

1920s, gave legal and administrative form to these distinctions. The law of the Qu'ran by definition could not apply to non-Muslims and thus religious minorities required separate arrangements (Laponce 1960: 84). The millet system divided society into communities along religious lines, with each non-Muslim individual or group belonging to one millet or another (Orthodox, Armenian, Catholic or Jewish) according to their religious affiliation. As a result, each non-Muslim religious community was given substantial autonomy with regard to education and property as well as religious affairs.

Arguably these category distinctions reflect the different perceptions of threat applied to each type of religious minority within the universitas. The risks associated with non-members are generally those of disloyalty towards the universitas due to their alternative belief systems, or erosion of the universitas, especially when proselytism is practised – in which case, of course, the problem of non-membership becomes entangled with the problem of lapsed membership. In contrast, the threat associated with lapsed members is almost always that of subversion. To reiterate, in circumstances of religious universitas, the values of the religious community are also those of the political community; religious dissent thus becomes political dissent. If religious conformity is not maintained, then political stability may be jeopardized. Whereas disloyalty suggests a failure to comply fully with laws and practices, subversion evokes the deliberate attempt to overthrow the entire legal and political structure. Thus the challenge posed by lapsed members is more fundamental and far-reaching than that posed by non-members. A brief comparison of the treatment accorded to Jews and Christian heretics in medieval Europe illustrates this point.

Jewish minorities were subject to a series of special requirements designed to limit their influence within and indeed upon the Catholic universitas. Since Jews were unable to take Christian oaths they were excluded from the feudal, manorial and guild systems. As a result, only a limited number of occupations remained open to them. Further restrictions on residence effectively confined Jews to particular areas ('ghettos') within European cities. Such practices may ostensibly have been for the protection of the Jewish minority but in reality were often intended to facilitate political control by the

Christian majority. Certainly they did little to prevent periodic attacks by Christians. The wave of anti-Semitic violence which spread across France and the Holy Roman Empire in the wake of the First Crusade's call to arms (in 1095) is a case in point: that episode culminated in massacres at Worms, Trier and Metz. Yet remarkably a Jewish presence was for a long while at least minimally tolerated because Jews provided useful economic services for the larger Christian community (as bankers, moneylenders, traders, doctors, etc.).

In contrast, heretics such as the Cathars by definition could not be tolerated. The Cathars (or Albigensians) considered themselves to be 'true Christians' or 'good Christians' as distinct from the Catholic Church, which in their view had betrayed the 'genuine' teachings of Jesus Christ (Ladurie 1979: viii). By 1200, Catharism had become widespread in the Languedoc, a situation which the Catholic authorities could not tolerate. The 1908 *Catholic Encyclopedia* nicely summarizes this medieval perspective: 'Christian Europe was so endangered by heresy . . . [that] it was, therefore, natural enough for the custodians of the existing order in Europe . . . to adopt repressive measures against such revolutionary teachings' (*Catholic Encyclopedia* 1908). In 1209, the barons of Northern France organized a crusade against the Cathars and the heretical movement was brutally suppressed.

At about the same time, the Catholic Church created an inquisitorial system designed to find, try and punish heretics. By 1240, the Inquisition had become a general institution in all lands under the purview of the pope. By the end of the thirteenth century, there were separate bureaucracies in each region of Catholic Christendom charged with ensuring its proper function. The procedures of the Inquisition gave a person suspected of heresy the right to confess and repent. Failing this, the accused was taken before the inquisitor, interrogated and tried. Torture was commonplace. On admission or conviction of guilt, a person could be sentenced to any of a wide variety of penalties, ranging from simple prayer and fasting to confiscation of property and imprisonment, including life imprisonment. Condemned heretics who refused to recant and those who relapsed after repentance received the death penalty (*Catholic Encyclopedia* 1908). This organized persecution is perhaps the most telling indication of how adverse Christian power was to religious dissent during the medieval period.

Religion and dynasty

The combined effects of the Renaissance and the Reformation fragmented the hitherto universalist structure of Catholic Christendom. The clear implication of the Protestant Reformation was that 'overarching religious uniformity, even at the theoretical level, was gone for good' (Cameron 1991: 198). Protestant theology 'disengaged the authority of the state from the overarching religious sanction of respublica Christiana' (Jackson 2000: 161). In so doing it encouraged secular princes to assert their dynastic prerogative to reform religious practices within their territories irrespective of papal sanction.

These changes were legitimized by the doctrine of the divine right of kings, which challenged the universalist claims of the papacy with a competing ideal of divinely appointed dynastic monarchs (Figgis 1922). While political authority was still derived from the Christian god, it was increasingly understood to be vested in a series of secular dynastic princes rather than in a single spiritual ruler. As a corollary of these changes, religion came within the purview of the prince and was used as a means of securing his dynastic power. England, for example, became Protestant under Henry VIII in order to ensure a male succession for the Tudor dynasty. The Church of England was later consolidated under Elizabeth I to protect against (Catholic) intervention from Spain and (Calvinist) subversion from Scotland. Elizabeth was compelled to enforce membership in the Church of England in order to preserve the territorial integrity of her kingdom from the threat of external attack (from Spain) and internal revolt (by Calvinists and Catholics). In other words, matters of faith, including the treatment of religious minorities, became inexorably linked with dynastic considerations.

Spain under the so-called 'Catholic Monarchs', Ferdinand and Isabella (1479–1516), provides a characteristic example of religious policies at work in the interest of dynastic consolidation. The union of the hitherto separate dynastic kingdoms of Aragon and Castile was effected in 1469 by Ferdinand of

Aragon's marriage to his cousin Isabella of Castile. Their joint reign was inaugurated with the promulgation of measures designed to strengthen royal authority over their newly unified kingdom. Insistence on religious conformity was a key component of their plans. In 1478, Ferdinand and Isabella obtained a papal bull from Pope Sixtus IV allowing them to establish a 'Spanish Inquisition' to deal with the perceived threat of lapsed Jewish converts to Christianity. In 1492, all those Jews who refused to be baptized – approximately 170,000 – were compelled to leave Spain and their remaining assets were forfeited to the Spanish crown (*Encyclopaedia Britannica* 2005c). Although ostensibly founded to further religious ends, the Inquisition in Spain became a 'crown institution' (Hayes 1904: 85). The central administration of the Spanish Inquisition increased dynastic control over previously separate feudal fiefdoms and in so doing effectively checked the power of the nobility.

While dynastic princes were prepared to act ruthlessly against those (including religious minorities) who challenged their new-found sovereign authority, their motivation tended to be self-interested rather than strictly theological. It is claimed, for example, that Henry VIII remained a Catholic at heart in spite of his political opposition to the papacy (Hayes 1904: 87–8). This fact perhaps explains why Henry could not understand the principled refusal of his friend and public servant, the devout Catholic Thomas More, to swear allegiance to the Act of Succession that nullified Henry's (Catholic) marriage to Catherine of Aragon and thus enabled Henry's subsequent (Protestant) marriage to Anne Boleyn. Indeed, from the dynastic perspective, Thomas More's assertion that he 'died the King's good servant but God's first' was, perhaps, the ultimate statement of disloyalty since it fundamentally disavowed the dynastic claim of sovereign supremacy (Ackroyd 1999: 394).

Ironically, this quintessentially self-interested dynastic perspective opened up the possibility for policies of toleration should circumstances make these politically expedient. That is precisely what happened in France towards the end of the sixteenth century. The 1598 Edict of Nantes was granted to the Huguenots by Henry IV with a view to preventing further civil war between Catholics and Protestants. This decree established freedom of conscience throughout France and gave Protestants freedom of worship in certain areas according to specified conditions. The rationale was entirely political. As Henry IV is reputed to have said, 'There must be no more distinction between Catholics and Huguenots, but all should be good Frenchmen' (Kamen 1967: 143).

Not surprisingly given its origins, compliance with the edict was also determined by dynastic calculations. Following the death of Henry IV in 1610, the balance of power in France between Protestants and Catholics shifted once again. Accordingly, the Nantes provisions were gradually eroded until the Edict of Fontainebleau finally revoked them in 1685. As a result, Protestant clerics were exiled, churches were destroyed and their congregations forced to convert to Catholicism or flee abroad. From the 1670s to the start of the eighteenth century, it is estimated that between 200,000 and 500,000 Huguenots left France in search of religious freedom elsewhere (Haddad 2004: 69).

Changing political contingencies were also behind the 1689 Act of Toleration in England. English politics in the seventeenth century were turbulent in the extreme. Civil war, the execution and restoration of kings and the establishment of a constitutional monarchy all took place within a space of less than fifty years. Religious policies altered with the political fortunes of those in power. During the interregnum between the execution of Charles I in 1649 and the Restoration of Charles II in 1660, Protestant dissent outside the established Church of England was mostly tolerated (Coffey 2000: 146–9). Following Charles II's return, the Act of Uniformity in 1662 pushed Presbyterians and Independents out of the Church of England (Coffey 2000: 209).

It was only the unexpected conversion of James II to Catholicism which forced Anglicans into an alliance with dissenting Protestants. The fear that Catholic despotism might take hold in England prompted disaffected Anglican notables to invite William of Orange (the king's Protestant son-in-law) to intervene. It is in this context that a policy of toleration towards mainstream Protestant dissenters arose. These 'recognized non-conformists' were free to build churches, conduct marriages and baptisms, proselytize and even rebut Anglicans in their sermons. Significantly, however, the 1689 act excluded anti-Trinitarian Protestants, Catholics, Jews and atheists, who were all judged to be potentially subversive towards the state (Coffey 2000: 199). Once again, political calculations were the crucial factor determining which religious minorities would be tolerated and which suppressed.

In sum, religion, like so much else in the dynastic state, was only politically salient to the extent that it facilitated or hindered the authority and ambitions of the prince. Where religious diversity conflicted with dynastic interest, it was firmly and often ruthlessly suppressed. However, where an alliance between religions was considered necessary to preserve the authority of the crown and its territorial possessions, policies of toleration towards religious minorities could sometimes be enacted.

Religion and nation

Until the eighteenth century, religion remained the foundation of political authority in Europe. Both the medieval Christian *universitas* and the dynastic states which succeeded it claimed to rule by virtue of a divinely sanctioned right. Religion was thus the final arbiter of political community. The doctrine of popular sovereignty changed all that – from the end of the eighteenth century onwards, ultimate political authority was thought to reside in 'the people', imagined as a self-determining 'nation', rather than the Christian god. But it would be wrong to conclude from this that the 'Age of Nationalism' was also an 'Age of Secularism' as some commentators have suggested (Gellner 1997: 77). Far from it: religious loyalties were tenacious and they held firm longer than most of those inherited from the dynastic period (Shafer 1955: 120).

What changed therefore was not so much a belief in religion per se but rather the political purposes applied to religious sentiment. Whereas previously religion had served the dynastic interests of sovereign princes, henceforth it would become a tool in the service of nation-building. So long as religion provided a convenient source of myths, memories and symbols around which an image of the nation could be constructed, it was useful and would be encouraged. But where religious loyalties threatened to weaken or divide the nation, they would be ignored or suppressed in the national interest.

Civic religion

One pattern of national development was for the nation-state to effectively 'nationalize' the dominant religion within its jurisdiction. Thus, for example, the Church of England remained the 'established' religion in the United Kingdom even after the dynastic principle had given way to parliamentary supremacy. Membership in the civic nation with all the attendant rights of political participation was thus contingent upon being a member of the Church of England. Consequently, religious dissenters (including various Protestant Christian sects as well as Catholics and Jews) were not only outside the Church of England but therefore also excluded from the English body politic.

In post-revolutionary France, too, religious institutions were increasingly co-opted by the state.

> During the Revolution the governing groups confiscated church property, declaring it part of the national patrimony and as such to be used for the benefit of the nation. In a Civil Constitution of the Clergy, the National Assembly made the clergymen national servants, forced them to swear 'to be faithful to the nation' and almost severed the connection of the Catholic priests with their 'universal' head, the Pope in Rome. (Shafer 1955: 120)

Similarly, while the individual right to freedom of opinion including religious belief was enshrined in the Declaration of the Rights of Man and of the Citizen (1789), such liberties extended only so far as these were compatible with the public good. Thus, article 10 of this declaration stipulates that 'No one shall be disquieted on account of his opinions, including his religious views, *provided* [italics added] their manifestation does not disturb the public order established by law.' We see this pattern repeated in many European countries where the dominant religion was incorporated into the institutional structure of the emerging nation-state. So, for example, it was reasonably commonplace for the official religion to be given civic responsibility for, among other things, the registration of births, deaths and marriages and related activities necessary for the identification of citizens and the acquisition of certain rights of citizenship. In these circumstances, the relationship between the official religion and the nation-state is such that religious minorities are controversial and may be viewed as a threat to civic institutions and public order.

British suspicion of Catholic loyalty to the pope in Rome and the fear that this might encourage subversive activities against the British state and its institutions is a case in point. Lord Liverpool, speaking in Parliament in 1818, nicely summarized these concerns:

> The main objects of the Catholics were to be allowed to sit in Parliament, in the privy council, and to be eligible to the great offices of the state . . . The principle of the constitution as established in 1688 was essentially Protestant; the connexion of a church and a limited monarchy was absolutely essential to the existence of civil liberty and of constitutional government; and in deciding the question that the King must be Protestant, they had also decided that the government must be Protestant likewise . . . The Roman Catholic not only brought a qualified allegiance, but differed from other dissenters in this, that he not only questioned the King's supremacy, but acknowledged a foreign one . . . It was not true . . . that the church of Rome exercised no power except in matters purely ecclesiastical. . . . There could be little doubt that if the Catholic hierarchy possessed the power, they would use that power in pursuit of farther objects, namely, for the attainment of at least a participation of the property enjoyed by the clergy of the established church. (UK *Parliamentary Debates*, vol. 40, 1819: cols 433–8)

Because of widespread anti-Catholic suspicions of this nature, the first Catholic Relief Act was not passed until 1778 (almost a century after the first Protestant 'non-conformists' had been given religious freedom). It allowed Roman Catholics in the United Kingdom to own property, inherit land and join the army subject to an oath against Stuart (the ousted Catholic dynasty) claims to the monarchy and the civil jurisdiction of the pope. Popular reaction against this legislation led to the Gordon Riots of 1780 in which a crowd of 50,000 marched on the Westminster Parliament demanding that the Relief Act be rescinded. As a result, full Catholic emancipation did not take place until 1829, and even now the Act of Settlement (1701) prevents Catholics from succeeding to the throne.

In sum, where one religion becomes incorporated into civic institutions the status of religious minorities will remain dependent upon public perceptions of threat. Where minority religions are considered benign, their adherents will be readily accepted into the body politic. However, where a minority religion is considered a risk to public order, its adherents may find their religious freedom limited or curtailed and their rights of citizenship correspondingly attenuated.

Ethnic religion

Another pattern of national development was for religion to become entangled in questions of ethnicity. Here the emphasis is not so much on an official religion determining eligibility for participation in civic institutions but rather religion determining ethnic belonging. Ethnicity denotes 'origin by birth or descent' (*OED* 1989) such that ethnic ties are imagined as ties of blood and cosanguinity. When religion becomes conflated with ethnicity, it is assumed that only members of a particular religion share in the imagined cosanguinity and blood ties may even become a criterion for religious membership (as in Judaism, where membership is usually inherited through matrilineal descent).

Religion is most likely to acquire this deterministic role in those circumstances where other ascriptive ethnic characteristics (such as language or race) are insufficiently distinct to differentiate effectively between populations. Thus, for example, ethnic community in the former Yugoslavia is imagined along religious lines – to be a Croat is to be Catholic, to be a Serb is to Serbian Orthodox, to be a Bosniak or a Kosovar is to be Muslim. During the Yugoslav wars of secession, religion was often used to identify ethnic minorities and single them out for discriminatory practices. Such attitudes led to religious institutions being the target of violence. Incidents like these still occur, particularly in war-affected areas like the Krajina in Croatia or Kosovo in Serbia-Montenegro where there are persistent reports of vandalism directed against the buildings and cemeteries belonging to minority communities (US Department of State 2003a; 2003c).

In such circumstances, religious minorities are by definition excluded from the ethnic nation – in other words, no legislation analogous to the various Catholic Relief Acts of eighteenth and nineteenth century Britain or other civic initiatives of this kind can incorporate them into the ethnic nation; instead, ethnic membership can only be acquired by entering into the imagined cosanguinity, for instance by religious conversion or some equivalent action of this kind. Accordingly, the members of such religious minorities are likely to find themselves in a permanently precarious position, especially where the ethnic nation controls the state.

Religious minorities may be denied equal access to public resources and experience other forms of officially sanctioned discrimination. For example, while Israeli law calls for freedom of religious worship, which is generally respected, the government provides lower quality education, housing, employment, and social services to non-Jews. On a per capita basis, the government spends a third less on non-Jews than on Jews (US Department of State 2003b). Although such policies are based on a variety of factors, they reflect 'de facto discrimination against the country's non-Jewish citizens' (US Department of State 2003b).

In extreme circumstances, religious minorities may even find themselves subject to official policies of persecution. Saudi Arabia is a case in point. Islam is the official religion there, and all citizens must be Muslim. The Saudi government limits the practice of all but the officially sanctioned version of Islam and prohibits the public practice of other religions. Accordingly, non-Muslim worshippers risk 'arrest, imprisonment, lashing, deportation, and sometimes torture for engaging in religious activity that attracts official attention' (US Department of State 2003d).

In sum, where religion defines ethnicity, religious minorities will remain outside the ethnic nation. For this reason, their continued presence within the territory of the ethnic nation-state is likely to be viewed as a prima facie threat to public order and stability. Accordingly, the members of religious minorities may find their religious freedom curtailed. At best, their access to public institutions may be limited and at worse they could find themselves not only excluded from the body politic but also subject to random acts of violence or state-sponsored persecution.

Religion and empire

Just as religion could provide political justification for the emergence of dynastic states, it could also be used to fashion arguments for imperial rule. Universalist religions like Christianity and Islam which aspire towards a global inclusion are particularly well suited to support imperial ambitions. The religious duty to enlarge the community of the faithful can readily be combined with territorial expansion. Islam, for example, inspired the Abbasid Empire (750–1258), the Ottoman Empire (1517–1922) and the Moghul Empire (1526–1857). But arguably it is in the various European overseas empires that the connection between universalist religion and imperial rule is most apparent.

From the outset, Christians sought to bring the 'good news' of Jesus Christ to all those who were still 'living in ignorance' of his message. This missionary spirit is already apparent in the activities of the early Christian Church where various 'saints' undertook to bring Christianity to pagan peoples in lands far removed from the See of St Peter in Rome – St Patrick in Ireland, St Augustine of Canterbury in England, St Cyril and St Methodius in Bulgaria and so forth. Christianity was therefore particularly well placed to provide an ideological justification for European overseas ambitions from the end of the fifteenth century until the middle of the twentieth.

As a result, Europeans imagined empire as much more than a self-seeking enterprise of trade and conquest for their own benefit; for them, empire was also a self-sacrificing act intended for the betterment of native populations. For more than four hundred years, Christianity accompanied the spread of European empire in the non-European world. Wherever the conquerors and the traders went, the Christian missionaries followed: 'Priests and friars travelled in all the Portuguese voyages and accompanied all the conquering Spanish armies . . . Calvinist ministers travelled into Dutch Asia and Africa . . . Anglican clergymen – and even a few women – followed the [British] flag into India and then into Uganda and Nyasaland and what became Rhodesia' (Pagden 2001: 63–4).

For many non-European peoples, their first exposure to European civilization was in the form of Christian beliefs and traditions. Christian mission schools in Africa, Asia and the

Americas did not confine themselves to Christian religious instruction but also taught European languages and western cultural values. In general, the intention of missionary activity of this kind was not simply to convert the native population to Christianity but also to assimilate them into European civilization. Some missionaries were critical of efforts to Europeanize the native population, condemning such attempts for spreading European vices such as alcohol, guns and tobacco while they purported to teach supposedly European virtues like hard work, thriftiness and an obedience to law. Father Libermann, founder of the Saint-Coeur de Marie (an order of missionaries dedicated to Africa), went so far as to instruct his staff: 'Do not judge according to what you have seen in Europe; lay aside the mores and spirit of Europe; become Negroes with the Negroes' (Cohen 2003: 276). But the majority believed that Christianity could best be spread through a broader 'civilizing project' which in turn necessitated the expansion of European political power (Cohen 2003: 277). In this way, Christian missionaries in Africa and Asia became in effect the agents of empire.

Yet because of its universalist ethic, Christianity also held out the possibility that through religion and its attendant civilizational values non-Europeans could eventually obtain a more equal relationship with their colonial overlords – for in so far as Christianity itself is concerned, community is based on creed rather than colour. In principle, therefore, not only is membership open to all but there is no moral basis on which to distinguish between an English Christian and an African Christian – all are 'brothers and sisters in Christ'.

This Christian progressivism was echoed by many colonial officials and political commentators throughout Western Europe, who believed that the direction of history was towards the increasing perfection of humankind. Accordingly, the general expectation was that the distance separating the 'civilized' nations of Europe from the 'backward' peoples of Africa and Asia would eventually disappear. From this perspective, the activities of Christian missionaries in Africa and Asia were directly contributing to the so-called 'progress of history'.

It should therefore come as no surprise that the ultimate impact of Christianity on European overseas empire was to encourage its eventual demise. Christian doctrine contains within it an inherent critique of empire.

Christ's message with its insistence on the priority of the spiritual over the temporal remained to be read, for all those who could do so. The religious orders in particular were inclined, to the displeasure not only of their secular overlords but also of their own superiors, to insist that it should be taken seriously and literally, that 'Love thy neighbour as thyself' should be a real deterrent against pillage and the unwarranted expropriation of the goods of others, even when, as was generally the case, those others were not Christians. (Pagden 2001: 64–5)

It was not long before the subject peoples themselves began to make a similar connection. Christian Africans, for example, came to identify themselves with the biblical 'children of Israel' and the British, French and Belgians with those who oppressed the Israelites, namely the 'Egyptians', 'Philistines' and 'Romans' (Hodgkin 1957: 97).

Eventually, Christians of both European and non-European origins began to question the moral arguments for denying self-rule to Africans and Asians. The Judeo-Christian approach to history lends itself to an interpretation of imperialism as a 'conflict between technical and military power and a moral idea, in which the eventual triumph of the moral idea is historically necessary' (Hodgkin 1957: 97). As Sir Charles Lucas put it in 1921: 'If you give freedom and education and the Christian religion to coloured men . . . you cannot confine them to a future of permanent subordination' (Lucas 1922: 207).

Religion and multiculturalism

The affirmation of religious diversity as distinct from the realist acceptance of toleration for the sake of political stability or economic gain was historically slower to develop. Nevertheless there were already proponents of religious liberty as early as the seventeenth century. At about this time, humanism merged with radical Protestantism and the Enlightenment to encourage scepticism towards religious dogma and the value of conformity.

Most of those who participated in the resulting debate – including Diderot, Voltaire, Locke and Pufendorf – advocated a limited religious toleration as distinct from unfettered religious freedom: however, a couple of notable exceptions stand out. William Penn, for example believed that limitations on religious freedom were both 'illegal and unconstitutional since the original contract between people and government laid down no condition that all the people must conform in religion in order to share civil rights' (Kamen 1967: 207). Penn later founded a multi-religious society in the American colony known as Pennsylvania where Catholics, Lutherans, Anglicans, Presbyterians, Baptists and Jews all managed to live together in peace despite the politics of intolerance which predominated elsewhere (Coffey 2000: 207). Similarly, Baruch Spinoza in his 1670 *Tractatus Theologico-Politicus* located the right of judging and interpreting religion within each individual man because he believed religion was both private and personal (Kamen 1967: 220). Spinoza argued that the state should be a 'peace-keeper in religion' by not favouring one religious faith over any other and took as his model Amsterdam where the adherents of different religious beliefs lived together in a condition of peace (Kamen 1967: 220).

In 1789, these intellectual traditions culminated in the first constitutional recognition of a right to freedom of religion. That year, the first amendment to the United States Constitution was proposed (and subsequently ratified in 1791). It ensured that 'Congress shall make no law respecting an establishment of religion, or prohibiting the free exercise thereof; or abridging the freedom of speech, or of the press; or the right of the people peaceably to assemble, and to petition the Government for a redress of grievances.'

The American policy of separation between religion and state was to a certain extent a political expediency made necessary by the religious diversity within the United States.

> In some of the states, episcopalians constituted the predominant sect; in others presbyterians; in others, congregationalists; in others, quakers; and in others again, there was a close numerical rivalry among contending sects. It was impossible, that there should not arise perpetual strife and perpetual jealousy on the subject of ecclesiastical ascendancy, if the national government were left free to create a religious establishment. The only security was in extirpating the power. (Story 1833: 1873)

But to incorporate that policy within the constitution along with a general right to freedom of religion was undeniably a crucial development in the slow movement towards multiculturalism.

The affirmation of religious diversity can take many juridical forms. In some countries, an established church exists alongside various recognized religions (as in Denmark and the United Kingdom), in others a position of state neutrality between religions is accompanied by a practice of legal recognition (as in Spain and Italy), while elsewhere a policy of separation between state and religion is maintained (as in the United States and Canada). What distinguishes a multicultural approach to religion is the state's willingness to accommodate such diversity while maintaining a position of neutrality between competing beliefs. No religion is singled out for special treatment and none are denied equal consideration.

More importantly, multiculturalism aims to encourage understanding and respect towards the wide array of religious beliefs and practices within the population. So, for example, a multicultural educational programme is likely to incorporate instruction in the beliefs and practices of the diverse religious traditions to be found among its citizenry. Thus, in October 2004, the United Kingdom's Education Secretary acknowledged that the views of religious and non-religious pupils should be treated with equal respect. Accordingly, the 2004 framework for religious education in the United Kingdom calls for children to study the six main religions within British society – Christianity, Buddhism, Hinduism, Islam, Judaism and Sikhism – but also other religious traditions such as Baha'i, Jainism and Zoroastrianism, as well as secular philosophies such as humanism (*The Independent*, 29 October 2004).

Multiculturalism, however, cannot prevent religious diversity dilemmas from arising. In the early 1990s, after almost thirty years of multicultural programmes and policies, Canadian public opinion was deeply divided over whether Baltej Singh Dhillon had a right to wear his (Sikh) turban with the ceremonial red serge dress uniform of the Royal Canadian Mounted Police instead of the usual flat-rimmed hat. His right was eventually upheld by the Supreme Court of Canada on the basis of both the freedom of religion and multiculturalism provisions of the Canadian Charter of Rights and Freedoms (1982). Nevertheless, protests against this judgment were received from over 195,000 Canadians who claimed that 'mounties' wearing turbans undermined a potent symbol of Canadian identity (SikhSpectrum.com 2002).

Nor can multiculturalism guarantee that the rights of religious minorities will always trump competing public interests. In January 2003, for example, members of the London Metropolitan Police stormed and searched Finsbury Park Mosque following the discovery of the toxin ricin in a North London flat. The British government defended this action as part of its response to the post-September 11 terrorist threat. Officials claimed that the police remained sensitive to Muslim beliefs and practice throughout the operation, taking care to stay outside the prayer room and wear plastic coverings over their shoes. Nevertheless, this incident caused widespread outrage amongst the United Kingdom's Muslim community who, notwithstanding the British state's publicly declared commitment to multiculturalism, generally viewed it as an affront to their religious dignity (BBC News 2003).

Multiculturalism does not preclude a state acting in defence of the public good, whether this is defined in terms of preserving national symbols or preventing terrorists threats or on some other basis. Nor can it prevent feelings of unease or even resentment amongst the minority so effected. But multiculturalism arguably increases the likelihood that hard choices like these will only be decided by due legal process and consideration of minority sensibilities.

Religion between communities

Religion enters into relations between communities as an extension of internal attitudes towards religious diversity. Where a political community is understood to be synonymous with a particular religious community, external relations will reflect religious values and aspirations – wars are likely to be fought for reasons of faith, territories may be acquired to protect holy sites and co-religionists, diplomacy will become entangled in theology and so forth. In contrast, where a political community is imagined as distinct from religious community then religious considerations are less likely to affect external relations.

Conflict between religious universitae

The starting point for relations between religious universitae is one of continual fear and misapprehension owing to the religious differences between them. Accordingly, the general expectation is for conflict rather than coexistence (Bozeman 1960: 236). Moreover, in this world view, international relations are by definition relations with non-believers and thus subject to perfidy. In such circumstances, the basic principles of an international society – mutual recognition, common norms and shared practices – are unlikely to develop. The imagined space between universitae is thus a sphere of anarchy and not society. Traditional Islamic thought powerfully expresses this religious universalist world view when it distinguishes the 'sphere of Islam' from the rest of the world, which is a 'sphere of war' (Bruce 2000: 45).

From the perspective of a religious universitas, international relations are characterized by a relentless struggle for religious beliefs and adherents which will only be overcome when one religion ultimately prevails over all others and humankind is united within a global universitas (Bruce 2000: 45). Within this struggle, three types of activity directed at the problem of religious diversity beyond the universitas emerge: religious war, missionary activity and a concern for co-religionists in lands governed by non-believers.

Religious warfare has two primary functions: to maintain the religious homogeneity within the existing borders of the universitas; and through conquest to help it achieve its manifest destiny as the ultimate community of humankind. In Catholic Christendom, the crusades reflect this spirit of religious warfare and were waged in the name of Jesus Christ for the defence of Catholic doctrine, the safety of the Catholic universitas, and the liberation of sacred Christian sites and Christian co-religionists from Muslim rule (Bozeman 1960: 272). Although primarily directed against Islamic power in the Middle East, there was also an internal Christian aspect to the crusades which is representative of the overlap between internal and external policies concerned with the problem of religious diversity. For it was also through the conduct of religious war that heretical sects such as the Cathars or Albigensians in the Languedoc were exterminated and the rival Christian universitas of Byzantinium temporarily overthrown.

In both the Christian and the Islamic traditions, it is not at all clear whether attempts to encourage conversion should be understood as a function of force or one of persuasion. The Muslim concern with purity of thought and deed in order to convert by example is evidence of this, as is the foundation of Christian religious orders such as the Franciscans (1209) and Dominicans (1214). As a result, we should distinguish between external relations conducted as religious warfare from those conducted as missionary activity. Within the territory of another universitas, such missions are likely to be perceived as fundamental security risks because the converts of one universitas are in this scenario the other universitas' 'lapsed members'. The external practice of missionaries thus translates into the internal problem of subversion.

Religious minorities are a deliberate consequence of missionary activity. They are also an inadvertent result of religious warfare. In both cases, the status of co-religionists outside the territory of the related universitas is likely to become a subject of international relations. The existence of co-religionist communities may be either the pretext for or proximate cause of subsequent wars and missions. Alternatively, the treatment accorded to such groups may become the subject matter of communications between the universitas and other communities. There are medieval examples of communications between Christian and Islamic powers in the Middle East concerning religious (Christian) minorities. For example, in 1250 St Louis of France promised to protect the Maronite Christians in a letter to the local emir (Thornberry 1991: 27). But the position of co-religious minorities within the rival universitas can never be anything but uncertain due to mutual suspicion and rivalry.

Coexistence within international society

Contemporary norms of international relations have their origins in that political transformation which took place in Western Europe between the fifteenth and eighteenth centuries. During this period, not only did religious dissent become widespread within Latin Christendom but political and religious community itself became segmented into sovereign, territorial states due to the corresponding breakdown of the previous Catholic universitas. These changes were recognized and confirmed in the 1648 Peace of Westphalia, which restored order to Western Europe after thirty years of war between competing sovereigns and religious sects. As a result, several hundred previously subordinate territorial units of the Holy Roman Empire acquired the rights and privileges of sovereignty (Jackson 2000: 163).

At about the same time, an international society emerged to provide a permanent framework for the relations between these newly sovereign territorial communities. An international society is 'a group of states, conscious of certain common interests and common values [who] form a society in the sense that they conceive themselves to be bound by a common set of rules in their relations with one another and share in the workings of common institutions' (Bull 1977: 13). A society necessitates the mutual recognition of diversity among its members. It would be impossible to have an international society unless each state recognized that every other state had the right to claim and enjoy its own sovereignty free from outside interference (Wight 1977: 135). Accordingly, many of the external practices of a universitas – including religious warfare and missions of conversion directed at other members of international society – became increasingly difficult to justify. Indeed, non-intervention in the religious affairs of other sovereign states quickly emerged as a *grund* norm for relations between members.

Following on from the 1555 Peace of Augsburg, religious affiliations were territorialized as the purview of each individual sovereign. According to the principle of *cujus regio, ejus religio* (like sovereign, like religion), princes determined the religious practices within their territories. Subjects either complied with the established religion of the sovereign or migrated to another sovereign jurisdiction where their religious beliefs prevailed. An extensive transfer of populations within Germany followed (Watson 1992: 173). These migrations of religious dissenters reinforced both the doctrine of *cujus regio, ejus religio* and the prevailing assumption that religious homogeneity within the state ought properly to be maintained. Thus, to the extent that religious freedom was recognized within the Westphalian settlement, it was the freedom of the sovereign rather than the individual which prevailed (Evans 1997: 50).

Treaties, transferred territories and religious minorities

Initially, problems of religious diversity entered into international relations only when territories were transferred between members of international society. This is fully in keeping with a territorialized politics of religion since such transfers were potential threats to the geographic status quo recognized at Westphalia and, by extension, to international peace and stability. There thus emerged the general expectation that when territories were ceded by one sovereign to another, the pre-existing religious status quo within this geographic area would be maintained regardless of the religious convictions of the new prince. Lands that were Protestant would remain Protestant; lands that were Catholic would remain Catholic.

All of the major treaties of the seventeenth and eighteenth centuries, including the treaties of Oliva (1660), Nijmegen (1678), Utrecht (1713), Breslau (1742), Dresden (1745), Hubertusburg (1763), Paris (1763) and Warsaw (1772), contain such guarantees (Laponce 1960: 23–4). So, for example, the 'cities of Royal Prussia' ceded to Sweden in 1650 were guaranteed 'all the rights, liberties and privileges which they enjoyed prior to the war either in the ecclesiastical or in the lay domain' (Laponce 1960: 24). Similarly, the Treaty of Dresden (1745) ensured that the Protestant religion would be maintained in the territories of the two signatories (the Prussian Kingdom and the Habsburg Empire) 'without it ever being possible to introduce the slightest innovation' (Laponce 1960: 24).

Such religious guarantees, however, did not extend beyond the geographic confines of the transferred territory. So when George III of Great Britain gave Roman Catholics in lands formerly belonging to France the freedom to practise their religion (under the terms of the Treaty of Paris 1763), Catholics within the British Isles acquired no such rights. The treaty itself specifically referred to the 'inhabitants of Canada' and noted that it was only 'his new Roman Catholic subjects' who were permitted to 'practise their religion according to the ritual of the Roman Church' but with the proviso 'in so far as the laws of Great Britain permit' (Laponce 1960: 24). Consequently, these seventeenth and eighteenth century treaty provisions should not be interpreted as evidence of an international norm in favour of religious freedom per se.

The practice of linking boundary changes with religious guarantees for any minorities created as a result of territorial readjustments continued into the nineteenth and twentieth centuries. The Final Act of the Congress of Vienna included provisions for Catholics in territories transferred from Savoy to the canton of Geneva and in the Austrian Netherlands (Belgium) which were merged with the United Provinces (Holland) to create the Kingdom of the Netherlands under the rule of the (Protestant) House of Orange (Laponce 1960: 26). Eventually, similar guarantees were included in those treaties which recognized new or enlarged states in the Balkan peninsula as well as in Central and Eastern Europe (see pp. 46–9). It is worth mentioning here that as ideas of national self-determination took hold, the rights protected in international agreements like these continued to be largely religious but the groups so recognized increasingly became thought of as 'national minorities'. These developments are discussed more fully in the chapter on ethnicity.

Religion and the 'standard of civilization'

International relations with those rulers and peoples outside the still principally West European society of states were qualitatively different. Such relations were not predicated upon mutual recognition and sovereign equality but rather 'unequal treaty, capitulation and protectorate systems all with extra-territorial provisions' (Gong 1984: 8). In other words, the imagined space beyond the West European society of states remained an anarchic no man's land in which European interests and rivalries could be pursued largely unhindered by the emerging pluralist norms of international society.

Instead, a revised universalism often referred to as the 'standard of civilization' continued to operate in extra-European affairs. This standard incorporated many of the beliefs and aspirations of the old Christian universitas, including a desire to protect and promote the Christian religion in non-Christian lands. The principle of *cujus regio, ejus religio* did not apply to such territories and so the status of Christian co-religionists and missionaries remained a legitimate subject of relations with non-Europeans.

For example, several agreements between Christian powers and the Sublime Porte included specific guarantees for Christian minorities within Ottoman territories. There were already stipulations in the 1615 Austro-Ottoman Treaty guaranteeing good treatment and the right to build churches and practise their religion to Christians of all denominations living under the authority of the Porte in the Balkans and elsewhere (Thornberry 1991: 29). The rights of the Catholic Church were further secured in the Treaty of Carlowitz (1699) and the Treaty of Passarowitz (1718) which confirmed and extended the earlier provisions. These treaties guaranteed that 'Those who profess to be the people of Jesus Christ and who Obey the Pope . . . will have the right to build churches . . . Read the Scriptures, meet in assembly, [and] offer the divine Service' (Laponce 1960: 25). Similar provisions were made for the Orthodox churches in the Treaty of Kutschuk-Kainardji (1774). Unlike the agreements between West European sovereigns cited earlier, these provisions were not confined to particular areas but instead included the entire jurisdiction of the Ottomans. Moreover, they were understood to include a right of intercession in Ottoman affairs with respect to Christian interests. The right of intercession was later interpreted as a right of intervention (Evans 1997: 64).

Christian missionary activity and the freedom of worship for Christian minorities (whether European or native) was a defining feature of the spread of European power in Africa and Asia through trade and empire. As European relations with the non-European world were increasingly formalized in the transition towards empire, Christian freedom to worship and to proselytize was secured through treaties and consular agreements (Gong 1984). The 'unequal treaties' imposed upon nineteenth-century China following its defeat in the Opium War are a case in point. The 1858 Treaty of Tientsin signed by China under the threat of renewed Western military hostilities included a commitment to respect the religious freedoms of Christians both Protestant and Catholic, Chinese and European (Jackson Preece 1998b: 64).

It should be stressed that these guarantees were not concerned with the freedom of religion per se (which would include an equal respect for native beliefs and customs) but only with special privileges for the Christian religion and its adherents. The memory of this historic connection between European imperialism and Christian proselytism continues to be a potent source of suspicion towards Christian minorities in many parts of the world.

Religious minorities and the expansion of international society

By the middle of the nineteenth century, a respect for religious freedom had become a fundamental principle of the still predominantly West European international society (Claude 1955: 7). As this society began to expand, guarantees for religious minorities became a criterion for the recognition of new states. These international undertakings provided for both the free practice of religion and protection against discrimination on religious grounds. Moreover, the minorities concerned no longer reflected the historic European desire to protect co-religionists but also included non-Christians (including both Muslims and Jews). In this way, the requirements of religious freedom entered into public international law.

The Third Protocol of the 1830 London Conference preserved the rights of Muslims within the territory of the new Greek state and stipulated that all Greek subjects were to be 'eligible for public employment on a footing of perfect equality, without regard to difference of creed, in their relations, religious, civil or political' (as cited in Evans 1997: 66). Following this, in 1878 the Congress of Berlin decided that henceforth all 'prospective members of the European family of states' should confirm their allegiance to the principle of religious freedom as an indication of their respect for 'the principles which are the basis of social organization in all States of Europe' (Claude 1955: 6). Accordingly, the subsequent Treaty of Berlin (1878) linked the recognition of Montenegro, Serbia, Romania and

Bulgaria with religious undertakings. As conditions of their independence, these states were bound to respect the freedom of religious minorities in their territories and to ensure non-discrimination between the adherents of different religions in civil and political rights, public office and membership in the professions and in industry (Jackson Preece 1998b: 65). Measures to ensure compliance were not formally included in the treaty itself. However, Innes Claude maintains that the great powers 'undoubtedly considered the Treaty of Berlin gave them a right of intervention in cases of non-fulfilment' (Claude 1955: 8–9). Such intervention did take place to rectify Romanian mistreatment of the Jewish minority (Claude 1955: 8–9).

The great powers' response to the emergence of new states in the Balkans established a standard of treatment that was later applied to Central and East European states after World War I (Jackson Preece 1998b: 67). These states were diverse in ethnicity, language and religion despite efforts to use the principle of national self-determination as a basis for delineating the new frontiers. As the so-called Committee on New States charged with redrawing the political map of Europe quickly discovered, new boundaries unavoidably created new minorities. Thus an expanded series of minority provisions for citizenship, linguistic rights, cultural rights and equality of treatment as well as religious rights were included in the post-war agreements with new or enlarged states: Poland; Czechoslovakia; Romania; Kingdom of Serbs, Croats and Slovenes (later renamed Yugoslavia); and Greece. At the same time, Albania, Lithuania, Estonia, Latvia and – outside Europe – Iraq were obliged to accept similar obligations as a condition of their admission to the League of Nations (Jackson Preece 1998b: 68).

In so far as religion was concerned, these guarantees provided for the free exercise, both public and private, of any creed, religion or belief whose practices were not inconsistent with public order or public morals. They also specified that differences of religion (alongside language and race) would not prejudice any citizen's admission to public employments, functions and honours or exercise of professions and industries. In towns or districts where there was a considerable proportion of citizens belonging to religious minorities, these groups would receive an equitable share of public funds for education, religious and charitable purposes (Jackson Preece

1998b: 75). In addition, certain religious minorities deemed particularly vulnerable in their new states were singled out for special provisions (Jackson Preece 1998b: 76–7). Thus Jewish minorities in Poland, Romania and Greece received extra guarantees with respect to citizenship rights, language education provisions and respect for their Saturday Sabbath. Similarly, Muslims in Yugoslavia, Greece and Albania were granted additional guarantees with respect to Islamic family law, mosques, cemeteries and other pious Muslim foundations, and educational institutions. Finally, the earlier 1878 provisions relating to the non-Greek monastic communities of Mount Athos (namely the Russian, Serbian and Bulgarian monasteries) were confirmed (Jackson Preece 1998b: 77).

Guarantees for religious freedom were also included in the League of Nations Mandates System which was created after World War I to administer the colonial territories of the defeated German and Ottoman Empires until such time as the peoples concerned were deemed ready for independent statehood. Article 22 of the League of Nations Covenant (1919–24) stipulated the 'guarantee of religious freedom, subject only to the maintenance of public order'. Where domestic circumstances of religious diversity existed, additional requirements with respect to religious freedom were made. For example, the preamble of the Mandate for Palestine (granted to the United Kingdom in 1922) emphasized that it was 'clearly understood that nothing should be done which might prejudice . . . civil and religious Rights . . .' The main body of the mandate agreement went on to specify provisions for the 'complete freedom of conscience and the free exercise of all forms of worship subject only to the maintenance of public order and morals' (article 15). The 'holy days' of all religious communities were to be recognized as legal days of rest (article 23) and free access to 'Holy places' guaranteed (article 13).

The United Nations Trusteeship System established after World War II to take over those responsibilities previously assigned under the League Mandates was predicated upon a similar commitment to 'encourage respect for human rights and fundamental freedoms for all without distinction as to race, sex, language or religion' (article 76, chapter XII, UN Charter). As with the previous mandates system, where religious diversity was potentially problematic, minority religious guarantees were recommended practice. For example, the 1947 General Assembly Resolution on the Future of Palestine contained a chapter entitled 'Religious and Minority Groups' which affirmed the principles of religious freedom and non-discrimination. Similar provisions were included in the Statute for the City of Jerusalem approved by the Trusteeship Council in 1950 (Jackson Preece 1998b: 107).

After 1960, however, independence became a pre-emptory right of certain categories of jurisdictions, regardless of their ethnic, religious or linguistic composition, and the guarantee of special provisions for religious and other minorities ceased to be a criterion for the recognition of statehood. The older practice of minority rights conditions was not revived until after the end of the Cold War and even then has been largely confined to Europe (Jackson Preece 1998b). Thus while European regional organizations, including the Council of Europe, the Organization for Security and Cooperation in Europe and the European Union, have made the provision of minority rights including guarantees for religious minorities a formal requirement for membership, other international organizations have yet to follow suit.

Religion and human rights

Instead, since 1945 the international concern for religious freedom has been mainly phrased in the language of human rights rather than in the language of specific minority guarantees. As early as 1941, President Roosevelt identified four fundamental freedoms as the basis for international cooperation after World War II: the freedom of speech and expression, the freedom of worship, freedom from want and freedom from fear. Freedom of religion was considered fundamental because it was presumed to be a criterion for democracy within states as well as peace between states (Sohn 1995).

The relationship posited between freedom of religion and democratic government was premised upon the historical experience of civic nation-states like the United States, France and the United Kingdom. In each of these cases, the progressive recognition of freedom of religion for larger and larger segments of the population had paralleled the development of representative institutions and the rights of citizenship. In contrast, totalitarian regimes like Nazi Germany were inclined to view independent religious organizations as a potential obstacle in their efforts to inculcate particular ideological beliefs amongst the population. For this reason, Hitler tried to establish an official German Reich Church in order to ensure the supremacy of the Nazi state over (Christian Protestant) religious organizations (Helmreich 1979).

Unlike the earlier guarantees for religious minorities, the human right to freedom of religion was not directed at the members of any particular community but instead understood as a universal right vested in every individual human being. The core normative content of the human right to freedom of religion may be found in article 18 of the Universal Declaration of Human Rights (UDHR) (1948) which affirms every individual's 'freedom to change his religion or belief, and freedom either alone or in community with others and in public or in private to manifest his religion or belief in teaching, practice, worship and observance'. This statement is echoed in article 18 of the ICCPR which adds the proviso that 'freedom to manifest religion or belief' may be subject to limitations but only those which are 'prescribed by law' and 'necessary to protect public safety, order, health, or morals' or 'the fundamental rights and freedoms of others' (ICCPR 18.3). Similar provisions intended to protect individual freedom of religion from incursions by the state can be found in article 9 of the European Convention on Human Rights (ECHR) (1950), article 12 of the American Convention on Human Rights (ACHR) (1969), and article 8 of the African Charter on Human and Peoples' Rights (commonly referred to as the 'Banjul Charter') (1981). In each of these texts, freedom of religion is recognized as a core civil liberty essential for democracy.

There is, however, an alternative interpretation of freedom of religion which may be found in the Cairo Declaration on Human Rights in Islam. Here the intention is not to promote democracy but to identify a discourse of human rights compatible with the main teachings of Islam. The rights elaborated in this context thus draw upon the Islamic Shari'ah rather than the political experience of western democracies. The Cairo Declaration affirms that 'all men are equal in terms of basic human dignity' and suggests that the 'true religion

[Islam] is the guarantee for enhancing such dignity'. 'Every human has a right to receive both religious and worldly education' with a view to 'enabling man to be acquainted with the religion of Islam' (article 9). Freedom to change religion is not mentioned. Instead, in a statement which recalls the historic connection between European imperialism and Christian proselytism, article 10 warns 'It is prohibited to exercise any form of pressure on man or to exploit his poverty or ignorance in order to force him to change his religion to another religion or to atheism.'

The disparities between the Islamic definition of religious freedom and the United Nations standards are indicative of a more general tension between the advocates of universal human rights and the proponents of cultural diversity (Brown 2002: 187–211). International controversy over the appropriate content of religious freedom is entangled in this larger, cultural debate about the relevance of purportedly western legal and political practices for non-western societies (Freeman 2002: 101–8). From the non-western perspective, local cultural and religious practices need to be protected from external influences which threaten to erode traditional ways of life. This view is fundamentally at odds with the position adopted by most human rights scholars, who assert the universal validity of freedom of religion and the other guarantees included in the main United Nations documents. Ironically, minorities are very often caught in the middle of these debates. On the one hand, minorities want to sustain their own traditional ways of life from encroachment by dominant local or indeed global practices. At the same time, however, they often view international standards as an important way to limit domestic incursions on their freedom. Given these various controversies, it is hardly surprising that domestic compliance has lagged behind international standard setting in the area of religious freedom.

To encourage greater respect for freedom of religion, in 1986 the United Nations Commission on Human Rights (UNCHR) established the office of the Special Rapporteur (SR) on Religious Intolerance, subsequently renamed the Special Rapporteur on Freedom of Religion or Belief. The Special Rapporteur's mandate is to identify incidents and government actions that are inconsistent with provisions for religious freedom. In 2001, the Special Rapporteur issued 85 communications (including one urgent appeal to the Islamic Republic of Iran) sent to 52 States (United Nations 2001). Problems of concern identified by the SR on Religious Freedom included the conviction and death sentence of members of the Baha'i faith in Iran because of their religious activities; the prohibition of altars and religious objects in private homes in Tibet; Eritrea's failure to recognize conscientious-objector status and the consequent arrest of Jehovah's Witnesses there; compulsory instruction in the Orthodox religion in Greek public schools; police refusal to protect Jehovah's witnesses from attack by an Orthodox mob in Tbilisi, Georgia; prohibition of conversions without prior authorization from the local police and the district magistrate in India's Orissa State; the conviction of a writer for blasphemy in Kuwait; and the destruction of churches and Christian-owned property in Indonesia (United Nations 2001).

This brief list of examples is sufficient to demonstrate that infringements of religious freedom are widespread and not confined to any particular geographic or cultural context. Equally, it is also self-evident that restrictions on religious freedom are almost always directed at religious minorities. Thus, while the right to freedom of religion has come to be framed in the language of universal human rights, the circumstances it seeks to address remain overwhelmingly a 'problem of religious minorities'.

The rights of religious minorities

The 'problem of religious minorities'

Religion is about much more than a belief in the divine; it is a way of living and as such has a fundamental bearing on human relations. This social aspect of religion is the key to understanding religious diversity dilemmas. Religion becomes controversial where the beliefs and practices it requires conflict with those of the political community. Where the political community is itself premised upon religion either because it is a theocracy (as were the medieval Catholic and Islamic universitae) or because the imagined cosanguinity of the ethnic nation is attributed to a particular religion (as in Israel), then religious minorities are by definition excluded from the body politic. In such circumstances, their continued existence within the territory of the political community is a prima facie threat and is likely to remain, at best, contingent. Where the political community is imagined along secular lines, as in a civic nation or a multicultural state, then religious minorities are not a prima facie threat and accordingly they are more likely to be tolerated by or accepted within the body politic. However, even under these more favourable conditions, the potential exists for religious beliefs and practices to conflict with the interests of the political community. Consequently, the 'problem of religious minorities' is usually experienced as an interference in the ability to live by one's religious convictions: it is very difficult to coerce beliefs, but the social practices which follow on from these beliefs can readily be disrupted or suppressed – religious institutions can be regulated or closed, religious Sabbaths may be curtailed or prevented by mandating specific working hours, items of dress such as headscarves and turbans can be declared unlawful, and so forth.

The minority rights response

The minority rights response to religious diversity seeks to encourage a social climate of acceptance towards religious minorities. This includes respect for religious freedom as well as protection against discrimination on the basis of religious belief or association. It also emphasizes the need to educate the larger community about the beliefs and practices of religious minorities so that these are less likely to be viewed with suspicion.

The right to believe

The right to believe speaks to the innermost convictions of the individual. This is a right of non-interference whereby the individual is free to believe, or indeed not to believe, according to his or her own conscience. Thus, for example, article 18 of the UDHR protects theistic, non-theistic and atheistic beliefs as well as the right not to profess any religion or belief. From this perspective, 'religion' and 'belief' are broadly understood such that the right to believe is not limited to traditional religions or to religions with institutional characteristics or practices analogous to those of traditional religions.

Such a broad interpretation is particularly important to minorities whose religious beliefs and practices differ fundamentally from those of the majority population. For example, the traditional religions of most indigenous peoples of the Americas are not organized or codified in the same way as Christianity or Islam but instead embody localized myths, memories and rituals which are often transmitted through oral storytelling. A broad interpretation of what constitutes 'religion' ensures that beliefs like these will receive equal protection alongside those of the so-called 'world religions' like Christianity and Islam.

Following on from this, the United Nations Human Rights Committee has ruled that the freedom to 'have or to adopt' a religion or belief necessarily entails the freedom to choose a religion or belief, including the right to replace one's current religion or belief with another or to adopt atheistic views. Article 18.2 of the ICCPR bans coercion that would impair the right to change religion or belief. This restriction includes policies that compel individuals to conform with majority orthodox religious beliefs, to convert to majority religions or to recant minority beliefs or religious affiliations. Policies or practices having the same intention or effect with respect to minority religions (for example by restricting access to education or medical care with a view to ensuring conformity with majority religions) are similarly inconsistent with article 18.2. A broad interpretation of the right to believe encompasses all these diverse circumstances and thereby seeks to ensure equality between the adherents of different religions.

The right to worship

The right to worship is extremely important for religious minorities because it introduces a communal element into the otherwise individual right to believe. This is acknowledged in the formulation of article 18 of the UDHR which specifically refers to religious freedom 'either alone or in community with others'. The act of worship is usually a collective practice in which a community of believers comes together to praise and beseech whatever power they hold to be divine – collective practices like these are performed every day in churches, mosques, synagogues and other holy places all over the world. The right to worship acknowledges that religious belief usually requires authentic community with fellow believers and aims to ensure that the form or extent of communal interaction should not be 'dictated, monitored or impaired by coercive requirements of the state' (Organization for Security and Cooperation in Europe 1999: 8).

The right to live in accordance with religious beliefs

The practice of religion is not confined to ceremony and ritual but also includes the building of places of worship, the use of ritual formulae and objects, the display of symbols and the observance of holidays and days of rest. It may require specific dietary practices, distinctive clothing or head coverings, participation in rituals associated with certain stages of life (e.g., birth, adolescence, maturity, etc.), the use of a particular language for liturgical purposes, and conscientious objection to military duties. And it usually necessitates the ability to train and choose religious leaders, establish religious institutions, provide religious education for children and other new adherents, and prepare and distribute religious texts or publications.

The minority rights response to freedom of religion requires states to respect the broad array of practices commensurate with a devout life as defined by the individual and the community to whom he or she belongs. Thus, for example, while the ICCPR does not explicitly refer to a right of conscientious objection, the UNCHR nevertheless believes that such a right can be derived from article '18. It therefore insists that where conscientious objection is recognized by law or practice, there shall be no differentiation between objectors on the basis of their particular beliefs. Similarly, it forbids discrimination against conscientious objectors because they have failed to perform military service. The minority rights response would hold states accountable to a similar standard of conduct in all other areas of life (education, dress, etc.) which can reasonably be said to result from religious convictions. This perspective would prohibit regulations such as the recent (2004) French law banning the prominent display of religious symbols by pupils in state-run schools.

The right not to be discriminated against or persecuted on the basis of religion

Finally, the minority rights response to religious diversity aims to prevent discrimination and persecution which result from religious belief or membership. Such treatment is obviously contrary to the general climate of acceptance towards religious diversity which minority rights proponents seek to establish. Discrimination against any religion or belief for any reason is explicitly prohibited under the terms of the Declaration on the Elimination of All Forms of Intolerance and of Discrimination Based on Religion or Belief (DEDR) (1981) as well as the general equality provisions of the UN Charter, the UDHR and the ICCPR. This protection extends to religions that are newly established within a state, or represent religious minorities that may be the subject of hostility on the part of the predominant religious community.

The UNCHR specifies that where a religion or set of beliefs is recognized as a state religion or is established as official or traditional or includes the majority of the population, it shall not result in any discrimination against adherents of other religions or non-believers. In particular, eligibility for government service cannot be restricted to members of the predominant religion nor can the state impose special restrictions on the practice of other faiths which are not in accordance with the prohibition of discrimination.

At the same time, article 20.2 of the ICCPR provides important safeguards against acts of violence or persecution directed towards religious minorities. According to article 20, no manifestation of religion or belief may amount to propaganda for war or advocacy of national, racial or religious hatred that constitutes incitement to discrimination, hostility or violence. Instead, states are under an obligation to enact laws to prohibit such acts.

Conclusion

The potential for religious diversity dilemmas is probably as old as human community itself. The desire to locate human experience in a larger cosmic plan and to explain the vicissitudes of human life by reference to a force greater than ourselves is so ubiquitous across both time and space that it may well be inherent within the human condition. This desire and the religious beliefs which follow on from it have a direct bearing not only on our private and personal thoughts but also on our human relations. It is this connection between religious belief and human conduct which makes religion a possible foundation for and thus also a possible rival to political community. Accordingly, religious diversity dilemmas are likely to be most acute in those circumstances where religion and politics overlap, as in a theocracy or in an ethnic nation-state which defines ethnicity on the basis of religion. But because religion has the power to shape ideas, identities and actions, the existence of religious minorities may still be controversial even where religion and politics are largely separate activities.

The 'problem of religious minorities' is thus usually experienced as an interference in the ability to live by one's religious convictions because these convictions are viewed as a threat to the prevailing political order. The minority rights response aims to limit such interference by encouraging a climate of acceptance towards religious diversity. From this perspective, religious diversity is not viewed as a prima facie threat to political order and, wherever possible, the political community is encouraged to accommodate the interests and concerns of religious minorities.

3
Race

Introduction

Race may be defined as 'each of the major divisions of humankind, having distinct physical characteristics' (*OED* 1989). In this usage, race is an invention of the eighteenth century intended to describe and classify humankind on the basis of observable hereditary traits such as pigmentation, stature and body shape. Race is thus a response to and indeed a recognition of human diversity which emerges out of the Enlightenment interest in categorization. Just as plants and animals could usefully be classified into biologically related genera and species, so too it was believed could humankind. Initially, race was a means of locating humankind within this natural order.

Race becomes problematic only where these descriptive and essentially arbitrary categories are imbued with political significance. Historically, such a connection between race and politics was not fully formulated until after the American and French revolutions successfully wrested political authority from the prince and gave it to the people. As an organizing principle both within and indeed between communities, race was most significant from the middle of the nineteenth century to the middle of the twentieth. Thereafter, racial ideas were increasingly rejected in favour of the principle of human equality.

Race as a diversity dilemma

Race emerges as a diversity dilemma once racial categories are understood to imply qualitative social and political differences between human groups. Those who hold such a view believe some races are 'superior' to others due to their alleged biological fitness or material or moral development. Once this transformation occurs, race becomes a hierarchical rather than merely a descriptive system. Such hierarchical assumptions have clear implications for social, economic and indeed political life. A belief in 'superiority' may translate into a putative right to rule over those considered less able. Similarly, assertions of 'inferiority' can become the justification for enforced or involuntary servitude. Racial categorization of this kind denigrates, disparages and in some situations even denies the dignity of individual human beings who are judged not in terms of their own actions and abilities but the prejudicial opinion of others. It may also condemn entire peoples to a 'subject status' where, instead of determining their own collective political existence, they are kept in thrall to outside powers. Misused in this hierarchical way, race is not only a source of inequality but also a denial of freedom.

Race within community

Race as an organizing principle within community distinguishes rulers from ruled. In other words, when race is used as a political principle it determines which groups ought properly to exercise authority within the community and which groups should be subject to that authority but excluded from participation in the decision-making process. It also establishes criteria, albeit vague and often contested, for assigning individual membership to what in effect become political and not merely physically descriptive categories.

Race and medieval universitas

Where religion is the organizing principle within community, as in the medieval Latin Christian universitas, ascriptive physical differences between individuals and groups have significance only to the extent that they are assumed to disclose the divine order. As previously indicated, in such circumstances religion rather than race, language or ethnicity is the key criterion distinguishing insiders from outsiders. In other words, the medieval universitas is a community of faith and not of ethnicity. What matters in this context is the human soul rather than the human body, which is merely a physical container and has little intrinsic value of its own. Accordingly, the modern, secular idea of race as indicative of a human rather than a divine order has no meaning in this context.

This is not to suggest that physical differences were unknown or ignored during the medieval period but rather that they were given a qualitatively different interpretation. Instead of seeking an explanation for the existence of diversity within nature (biology, climate, geographic location) or within human history (material and moral progress) as in the eighteenth and subsequent centuries, medieval Europeans looked to religion, and especially to the Christian Bible. In this context, the biblical story of the division of the world after the flood and the curse on Ham's posterity is particularly significant.

According to Genesis 9, the sons of Noah who came out of the ark after the great flood were Shem, Ham and Japheth. From them came all subsequent people, who were later scattered over the earth. Noah proceeded to plant a vineyard. When he drank some of its wine, he became drunk and lay naked inside his tent. Ham, the father of Canaan, saw his father's nakedness and went laughing to tell his two brothers. But Shem and Japheth covered their father's nakedness. When Noah awoke from his wine and discovered what had happened he prayed for the descendants of Shem and Japheth but cursed Ham's posterity. Noah said, 'Cursed be Canaan; a servant of servants shall he be unto his brethren. And he said, 'Blessed be the Lord God of Shem; and Canaan shall be his servant. God shall enlarge Japheth, and he shall dwell in the tents of Shem; and Canaan shall be his servant' (Genesis 9: 25–7).

Subsequent interpretation of this story by the Jewish general and historian Flavius Josephus in the first century AD associated the descendants of Japheth with Europe; the descendants of Shem with the Middle East and the Indian Ocean; and the descendants of Ham with Africa (Hannaford

1996: 91). Later still, Augustine gave the allegory a more explicit Christian meaning such that Shem represented the 'flesh of whom Christ was born', Japheth represented the Christian Church and Ham represented heresy (Hannaford 1996: 95). The darker pigmentation of Africans as compared to Europeans was thus popularly explained during the medieval period with reference to this Bible story as a divine mark placed upon the descendants of Canaan because of Ham's sin against Noah.

Yet crucially, regardless of their physical appearance, all humans were considered subject to a common, divinely sanctioned natural law and all were equally eligible for salvation through faith. This attitude towards diversity is apparent in the sixteenth century debate concerning the proper treatment of indigenous peoples within the so-called 'New World' purportedly 'discovered' by Christopher Columbus in 1492. To recall, the Catholic *universitas* was understood to be the embodiment of divine authority delegated by God to St Peter and the Vicarite of Jesus Christ. In principle, this rule was global and thus numerous papal bulls from the eleventh century onwards claimed authority over territories inhabited by non-Christians including, ultimately, the 'New World' itself. Similarly, the law of Christendom was seen as the embodiment of a divinely ordained natural law which in turn applied everywhere and to everyone, regardless of whether or not they were Christian.

It is precisely this Christian natural law tradition which the Dominican clerics Bartolomé de las Casas (1474–1566) and Francisco de Vitoria (1486–1546) cited in their attempt to moderate the worse excesses of Spanish conquest in the Americas (Anaya 2000: 9–13). Regardless of any physical, material or moral differences, both las Casas and Vitoria were adamant that the indigenous peoples of the Americas belonged to a common humanity and as such should not be deprived of liberty or property by force nor be reduced to slavery (Hannaford 1996: 149–50). According to las Casas and Vitoria, the people they referred to as 'Indians' not only had the same intrinsic, God-given worth as every other human being but were also potential members of the Christian community of faith and should be treated accordingly. Vitoria even went so far as to insist that discovery of the new lands across the Atlantic could not, in and of itself, confer title on the Spaniards 'anymore than if it had been they [the indigenous peoples of the Americas] who had discovered us' (Anaya 2000: 11). He was, however, prepared to sanction Spanish rule provided it was for the benefit of the indigenous population, whom he nevertheless considered 'unfit to found or administer a lawful State up to the standard required by human and civil claims' (Anaya 2000: 11). This assertion by Vitoria anticipates subsequent nineteenth and twentieth century arguments in support of European rule over less developed peoples in the interests of 'civilization'. It is nevertheless anachronistic to interpret statements like these in the context of later understandings of race because it was only after the Renaissance and Reformation that human existence came to be seen in secular terms. For so long as human experience was viewed as part of a divinely ordained plan, the positivist assumptions based on observable facts (whether biological or historical) integral to the modern understanding of race simply could not arise (Hannaford 1996: 147).

Race and dynasty

The word race did not enter West European languages until the period AD 1200–1500 and, even then, its early meaning had nothing to do with the organization of community (Hannaford 1996: 5). Instead, race referred to a 'contest of speed', a 'strong or rapid current' or 'the channel of a stream' (*OED* 1989). It was only during the fourteenth and fifteenth centuries that race began to acquire a political significance when it was sometimes used to describe the lineage or continuity of generations in royal or noble families (Hannaford 1996: 5).

This change in meaning corresponds with and indeed reflects a larger transformation in the organization of European community from the universitas of pope and Holy Roman Emperor to the segmented society of sovereign princes and their dynastic families. The idea of a noble 'race of kings' was very much in keeping with the emerging dynastic conception of political authority. From the fifteenth century onwards, princes increasingly based their claim to rule on the understanding that sovereignty was divinely vested in their person and, by extension, the particular dynastic lineage they represented – a doctrine which came to be known as the 'divine right of kings'. As this view of political authority took hold, kingship ceased to be determined by election or by coronation (Figgis 1922: 27). Instead, sovereignty became a hereditary entitlement vested in the next heir apparent. Thus the idea of a noble 'race of kings' set apart from ordinary men and women and with a God-given right to rule was well suited to the political aspirations of the great dynastic families such as the Tudors and the Valois during this pivotal transition from Catholic universitas to dynastic state.

Later on, the notion of race was extended to include not only dynastic families but the wider aristocracy of dukes, marquesses, earls, viscounts, barons, knights and esquires collectively known as 'gentlemen' as distinct from 'commoners' (a category which included citizens or burgesses, yeomen, labourers and husbandmen). Thus, for example, Raphael Holinshed's *Chronicles of England, Scotland and Ireland* (first published in 1577) distinguishes gentlemen by their 'race and blood' (Hannaford 1996: 173). Pierre Charon does likewise in his *De la sagesse* (first published in 1601) when he identifies the French nobility as gentlemen who belong to a 'race, house, familie carrying of long time the same name and the same profession' (Hannaford 1996: 175). Here it is perhaps important to recall that the earliest parliaments were the preserve of the nobility and so only 'gentlemen' were members of the political community over whom the sovereign presided. The extension of the category race to include gentlemen is an acknowledgement of their political status within the dynastic state.

This dynastic understanding of race has certain parallels with the modern social science concept. The emphasis on descent or lineage anticipates the biological interpretation of race as a consequence of cosanguinity; while the idea of a nobility set apart from and superior to ordinary men and women and with an intrinsic right to sovereignty or political participation foreshadows racial hierarchies of ruler and ruled. However, these similarities are little more than superficial and should not be taken out of the historical context in which they appear. In other words, the dynastic period is closer to but nevertheless still distinct from the modern era of popularly sovereign nation-states. This 'pre-idea' of race did not acquire a specific connotation distinct from that of *gens* (or clan) until the end of the seventeenth century (Hannaford 1996: 6). And it was only after the French and American revolutions successfully challenged the old dynastic order in the name of a new principle of popular sovereignty that the modern idea of race was fully conceptualized and indeed politicized.

Race and nation

Race-thinking 'entered the scene of active politics the moment the European peoples had prepared, and to a certain extent realized, the new body politic of the nation' (Arendt 1972: 161). The categorization of humanity into observable groups was increasingly salient in the context of the principle of popular sovereignty and its concomitant emphasis on popular identity. Once sovereignty was vested in the people, defining this category and membership within it became a matter of the utmost political urgency. Racial types which purported to organize humankind into groups according to a similarity of physical characteristics attributable to a common descent offered a readily available method of delineating one people from another and of determining which peoples were capable of exercising sovereignty. With its emphasis on physical characteristics, the idea of race would seem to fit the logic of ethnic nations but be inimical to the ideal of a civic nation. In practice, however, the appeal of race was not confined to ethnonationalists but extended to those who believed in the primacy of political institutions and experience over cultural, linguistic or indeed biological affinities. Nevertheless, the particular interpretation and political significance accorded to race continued to differ markedly as between what we might usefully call the civic progressive and the ethnic naturalist positions (Goldberg 2001: 74).

The civic progressive view of race   Civic nationalists believed race was politically relevant only to the extent that it paralleled and thus disclosed important material (economic and technological) and moral (legal, political and religious) differences in historical development between peoples. From this perspective, all humans had the same innate abilities.

What separated a 'savage' in the African jungle from the 'man on the Clapham omnibus' was the 'civilization' to which he belonged. Thus, in principle these differences could be overcome by tutelage or assimilation. In other words, ultimately all of humankind was advancing, albeit at various speeds, towards the same common goal which Hegel so evocatively termed the 'end of history'. Movement towards this destination was described as 'progress' and it was the duty of all 'civilized peoples' to assist those less far along than themselves. Lord Acton expresses this progressivist sentiment when he notes that 'inferior races are raised by living in political union with races intellectually superior' (Acton 1907: 290).

During the nineteenth and early twentieth centuries, the progressive view of history was crucial to debates on European overseas empire and international trusteeship. These points are discussed more fully later in this chapter. However, progressivist attitudes towards race may also be discerned in the domestic arrangements of so-called 'settler states' during this same period.

American and Canadian policies towards the indigenous population of North America provide useful examples of this trend. The progressivist thesis held that indigenous peoples should become more 'civilized' through their acquisition of the rule of law and political culture of the settler population (Goldberg 2001: 82). Accordingly, the idea of a civilizing mission was cited as justification for the practice of 'removals' (expulsion) to make way for new settlements, 'reserves' (segregation) where less developed peoples would be 'protected' from the worst excesses of modern 'civilization', and 'Indian schools' (assimilation) where indigenous children would acquire 'civilized' values in place of their more 'primitive' traditional customs.

Ultimately, 'white' settler states came to view their indigenous populations as 'domestic dependent nations' with a normative status comparable to 'colonial dependent nations'. As 'subject peoples', indigenous populations did not have the right to self-government or even consultation with respect to domestic policies directed at them. Where consultation occurred or consent was sought this was done on an ad hoc basis and was not intended to establish universal procedures. For example, while the notorious policy of 'Indian removals' to lands west of the Mississippi had the consent of the Choctaws of Georgia in 1830, very many tribes were subsequently forcibly transferred (Prucha 1997: 168–72). The long-term objective of these policies was the progressive development of the indigenous population with a view to their eventual entry into full political participation on the basis of equal citizenship. A hierarchical racial structure which distinguished 'white settlers' and their descendants from the indigenous population would persist only until this historic goal was realized. Thus civic nationalists who subscribed to progressive race thinking continued to believe in the primacy of political over sociological or indeed anthropological criteria in determining which peoples ought properly to exercise sovereignty through representative institutions. Racial categorization was a means to this end in that it helped establish criteria for identifying less developed peoples currently incapable of effective self-government and provided a paternalist justification for discriminatory policies directed at them.

The ethnic naturalist view of race   In contrast, the ethnic nationalists were inclined towards a more naturalist interpretation of race which was in keeping with their organic conception of community. From this perspective, race was a function of biology and so observable differences between racial groups reflected deeper and indeed more fundamental natural divisions within humankind. Race, alongside language, thus became one of the defining features of a purportedly 'genuine' ethnic nation as distinct from an 'artificial' political community.

The quest to identify and preserve ethnic nations proceeded in two closely related directions. While the philologists looked to linguistic genealogies and folklore traditions to establish ethnic affinities, biologists and physical anthropologists constructed ever more elaborate racial types on the basis of cranial size, skin and eye pigmentation, hair texture and other physical characteristics. Racial differences were identified not only between European, African, Asian and New World peoples but also within the 'native' European population, which was itself divided into Germanic, Mediterranean and Slavic sub-groups. The political implications of this racial categorization were enormous. Racial differences within existing states and empires became a further justification for those who aspired to redraw the political map on the basis of national self-determination.

Race also provided a convenient explanation for the rise and fall of communities throughout history. In *The Inequality of Human Races* (first published in 1853–5), Gobineau argued that 'degenerate . . . when applied to a people means (as it ought to mean) that the people has no longer the same blood in its veins, continual adulterations having gradually affected the quality of that blood' (Gobineau 1915: 25). In Gobineau's account, political arrangements have no effect whatsoever on the success or failure of a community. The decline and fall of the Roman Empire was not due to corruption or similar political failings but to a biological deterioration resulting from exogamy. The obvious interpretation of Gobineau's argument was that to survive and flourish, nations must remain racially 'pure'.

Such naturalist racial claims were given added credibility by Charles Darwin's account of the 'survival of the fittest' in the animal world and Herbert Spencer's analogy between societies and organisms (Vincent 1992: 241). The so-called 'social Darwinism' which resulted from the fusion of their ideas saw developmental differences between societies as the result of principles of natural selection which no amount of political tutelage could overcome. Civic progressives were considered to be fundamentally misguided in their beliefs because they failed to appreciate the inherent limitations of public policy in the face of unalterable natural differences.

> The belief, not only of the socialists but also of those so-called liberals . . . is that by due skill an ill-working humanity may be framed into well-working institutions. It is a delusion. The defective nature of citizens will show themselves in the bad acting of whatever social structure they are arranged into. There is no political alchemy by which you can get golden conduct out of leaden instincts. (Spencer 1969: 669–70)

Because politics could not alter nature, the only rational way forward was for politics to embrace nature. Communities flourished until they were weakened through contact with 'inferior' races or succumbed to competition from 'superior' races. The clear implication of these naturalist convictions was that 'superior' races required protection from the potentially 'degenerate' effects of social intercourse with those deemed 'inferior'. National self-determination thus became natural determinism such that the ideas of ethnic nation and biological race began to merge.

An ethnic nation was defined by ties of blood, language and cultural tradition; a race was defined by a similarity of physical, moral and intellectual characteristics resulting from common descent. Increasingly, therefore, membership in an ethnic nation was restricted to those who belonged to a particular race. The unity between racial membership and national membership is manifest in the Nazi Nuremberg Laws of 1935: article 2(1) of the Reich Citizenship Law defined a citizen as someone who is 'of German or kindred blood'; subsequent regulations further specified that a 'Jew cannot be a citizen of the Reich. He has no right to vote in political affairs and he cannot occupy public office.'

'Inferior races' constituted permanent minorities who would never be eligible for equal citizenship. From the ethnic naturalist perspective, the proper response to such minorities was separation and exclusion. These convictions motivated policies of segregation, laws against miscegenation, and racially defined immigration and citizenship criteria. Racist policies like these may be found in Nazi Germany, apartheid South Africa, and in the so-called 'Jim Crow' states of the southern United States prior to the 1960s.

Laws prohibiting interracial marriages (miscegenation) are a case in point. The 1935 Law for the Protection of German Blood and Honour forbade marriages and sexual relations between Jews and 'nationals of German or kindred blood'. Similarly, the 1949 Mixed Marriages Act in South Africa prohibited both interracial marriage and sexual relations. Anti-miscegenation laws continued to exist in the southern United States until 1967 when the US Supreme Court in *Loving v. Virginia* unanimously ruled them unconstitutional – at the time of this ruling, Virginia was one of sixteen states in which interracial marriage was a punishable offence.

Ethnic naturalist race thinking also inspired the so called 'science of eugenics' which in the interest of 'racial purity' and 'biological fitness' advocated selective breeding amongst the 'strong' combined with sterilization of the 'weak'. 'Positive eugenics' were facilitated through publicly funded marriage loans, child allowances and day-care facilities for the 'racially sound'. These measures are most closely associated with Nazi racial policies but the payment of 'baby bonuses' of various kinds was by no means confined to Germany. 'Negative eugenics' involving sterilization programmes were also a common feature of interwar policies directed at socially undesirable groups including racial minorities, the mentally ill, criminals and the poor and destitute. During this period, programmes for voluntary sterilization existed in the United States, Denmark, Switzerland, Sweden, Norway, Finland and Estonia as well as Germany (Mazowar 1998: 98). After the Nazi seizure of power in 1933, sterilization in Germany became compulsory for certain groups. By 1937, over 200,000 people had been forcibly sterilized there, including gypsies, the so-called 'Rhineland Bastards' (children of miscegenist relationships between German women and black French soldiers), the 'morally feeble minded', 'disorderly workers', 'the work-shy' and 'asocials' (Mazowar 1998: 99). Ultimately, of course, Hitler took this sort of ethnic naturalist race thinking to its ultimate extreme in his campaign of genocide against the Jewish and Roma minorities of Europe.

The dilemma of racial categories The arbitrary effects of race-thinking and the destructive consequences it can have on human lives are manifest in the application of racial categories. Idealized racial types only imperfectly correspond with the reality of human circumstances. As a result, supposed racial 'anomalies' are unavoidable. How, for example, should the dark-skinned child of two white parents be classified? That is exactly the dilemma which arose when Sandra Laing was born in apartheid South Africa during 1955. Expelled from her 'white' school because of her dark complexion and obliged to live as a 'coloured' child, Ms Laing was later reclassified as 'white' in 1967 when the law was changed such that the child of two 'white' parents could not belong to another racial group. But that did not make life any easier for Sandra Laing. Isolated and rejected by 'white' Afrikaaner society, Ms Laing fell in love with a black man, Petrus Zwane, with whom she eventually had two children. But 'officially' Sandra Laing could not live with her new family because apartheid law forbade different races from cohabitating. As a result,

Ms Laing spent years trying to change her racial classification to 'coloured' so that she could legally dwell with her son and daughter (*The Guardian*, 17 March 2003). Sandra Laing's life circumstances were fundamentally dictated by racial categories beyond her control whose arbitrariness is manifest in their changing content. As this tragic case demonstrates, ultimately racial membership is determined by law and politics, not science or social science.

The problem of definition is unavoidable in such circumstances, particularly as regards 'hard cases' which disclose the opaque and indeed amorphous boundaries between what are literally as well as figuratively intended as rigid 'black and white' categories. Consequently, citizenship and other legislation which uses 'race' to determine membership is notoriously inconsistent. For example, the original Reich Citizenship Law of 1935 established no criteria for determining who was and who was not a 'Jew' for purposes of the Act. While the problem had been discussed by Nazi party leaders, the civil servants who drafted the law failed to provide a clear definition. Eventually, a supplemental regulation was created to resolve this dilemma but it too was vague and did not (indeed arguably could not) adhere to strictly racial criteria. As a result, the 'Jewishness' of persons with mixed ancestry was assessed with reference to a combination of racial (descent) and religious (whether or not the individuals and their ancestors practised the Jewish faith) criteria. Not surprisingly, the administration of this regulation proved complicated because the necessary evidence on family background was difficult to locate. Bodies of 'family researchers' were employed to look into the matter but classification remained at best arbitrary.

Similar difficulties of racial classification are apparent in the context of the United States naturalization laws prior to World War II. In 1790, the United States Congress limited citizenship to 'free white men'. In the aftermath of the Civil War, citizenship was extended to 'aliens of African nativity and to persons of African descent'. Native Americans, as members of internal dependent nations, remained excluded from the rights of citizenship. But the eligibility of immigrants from beyond Western Europe for US naturalization was unclear. In the wake of growing and increasingly diverse immigration, by the end of the nineteenth century US courts were confronted with the problem of determining the 'whiteness' of would-be citizens. In 1894, for example, the Massachusetts Circuit Court ruled that unless explicitly stated otherwise, naturalization was limited to 'Caucasians'. But anomalies remained. How, for example, ought Syrians to be racially defined? In 1909 and 1910, the Massachusetts and Oregon District Courts respectively classified Syrians as 'Caucasians'. In 1913, however, the South Carolina Court denied Syrians the right to citizenship, arguing more generally that 'all inhabitants of Asia, Australia, the South Seas, the Malaysian Islands and territories, and of South America, who are not of European, or mixed European and African, descent' would be excluded from naturalization. In 1915, the US Supreme Court overturned this verdict as it applied to Syrians, citing as justification the fact that 'Syrians', 'Armenians' and 'Parsees' had been considered and treated as 'Caucasian' by US immigration law for the past fifty years (Goldberg 2001: 178–83). Cases such as these disclose the political dilemmas and personal tragedies which unavoidably arise when an invented concept such as 'race' is treated as a natural or material fact and becomes administratively codified within states.

Race and empire

Ideas of racial hierarchy are also apparent in the practice of European overseas empire. The legitimacy of empire was constructed in terms of the civic progressive view of history which judged the achievements of non-European peoples not in their own terms but according to prevailing European values. Against this European standard of civilization, 'non-European society could appear only as depraved, destitute and defective' (Bain 2003: 25). When the nineteenth century Whig historian in his London study looked towards Africa and Asia, he saw only 'despotic rule, endemic warfare, alien customs, and an absence of science, commerce and industry'; consequently, the peoples of Africa and Asia were 'typically derided as being filled with pride, passion and appetite' and 'ridiculed for their seeming preference of superstition to rationality, magic to science, and violence to law' (Bain 2003: 22).

The liberal consensus was that such 'inferior peoples' were

not yet 'beyond the period during which it is likely to be for their benefit that they should be conquered and held in subjection by foreigners' (Mill 1972: 377). Imperial rule was to be preferred 'if it is the one which in the existing state of civilization of the subject people most facilitates their transition to a higher stage of improvement' (Mill 1972: 382). Significantly, each of the major imperial powers justified their presence in overseas territories with reference to this 'civilizing mission'. 'The French endeavoured to civilize the "lower races" by assimilating them to the excellence of French culture; the Portuguese by introducing the Christian religion; the Belgians by imparting their religion and ideology; and the British by bringing their charges to self-government' (Bain 2003: 20).

Within the colonies themselves, the structure of community tended towards a racial caste system (Nicholls 1974). At the elite level, Europeans occupied the senior positions within the colonial administration and the local economy. Below them was a middle tier of lower level colonial officials, small business owners and professionals who served the needs of the non-European population. These individuals were distinguished from the rest of the native population by race (Asian in East Africa, Chinese in South East Asia and Anglo-Indian in India) or by civilization (as evidenced by a western education or Christian faith). The bottom of the hierarchy was filled by the majority of the native population who in the eyes of their colonial masters remained far removed from European civilization. Accordingly, this racial underclass provided the unskilled labour required to harvest those raw materials (coffee, tea, cocoa, copper, cotton, rubber, gold, diamonds and so forth) upon which the colonial economy depended.

Such racial division of power within the colonies was representative of both civic progressive and ethnic naturalist assumptions. On the whole, race determined an individual's position within colonial society. Limited upward mobility was possible but only for those rare individuals who demonstrated a closer affinity with European civilization. And even these fortunate few were barred from occupying senior positions of power (whether economic or governmental) by virtue of their membership in still 'dependent nations'. In other words, the possibility of social advancement remained open only so long as racial divisions continued intact. There was always a ceiling determined by race.

The basic presumption was that 'nature seems to intend the English [and similar European peoples] for a race of officers, to direct and guide the cheap labour of the Eastern People' (Dilke 1869: 192). Yet 'without race as a substitute for the nation, the scramble for Africa [and other overseas territories] . . . might well have remained a "purposeless dance of death and trade"' (Arendt 1972: 185). In much of the British Empire at least, civic progressivism constrained the worse aspects of imperial exploitation.

Such restraint was the deliberate intent of the so-called 'dual mandate' which sought to reconcile economic imperial self-interest with a more altruistic concern for local development. Lord Lugard, who formulated this key doctrine of British imperialism, did not deny that self-interest was involved but insisted that it could be reconciled with civic progressive ideals:

> Let it be admitted at the outset that European brains, capital and energy have not been, and never will be, expended in developing the resources of Africa from motives of pure philanthropy; that Europe is in Africa for the mutual benefit of her own industrial classes, and of the native races in their progress to a higher plane; that the benefit can be made reciprocal, and that it is the aim and desire of civilized administration to fulfil this dual mandate. (Lugard 1929: 615)

Where the dual mandate was more or less adhered to, the interests of the native population were understood to take precedence over the claims of European settlers. This opinion is explicitly stated in the Kenya White Paper of 1923: 'Primarily, Kenya is an African territory, and His Majesty's Government think it is necessary definitely to record their considered opinion that the interests of the African Natives must be paramount, and that if, and when, those interests and the interests of the immigrant races should conflict, the former shall prevail . . .' (quoted in Oldham 1924: 102). In stark contrast, where ethnic naturalist opinions triumphed the imperial experience came to resemble the Darwinian struggle of 'survival of the fittest'. As Hannah Arendt points out, this brutal attitude towards those deemed 'inferior races' resulted in terrible massacres of the native population: 'the Boer's extermination of the Hottentot tribes, the wild murdering by Carl Peters in German Southeast Africa, [and] the decimation of the peaceful Congo population – from 20 to 40 million reduced to 8 million people . . .' (Arendt 1972: 185).

Regardless of whether or not imperialism reflected a more moderate civil progressive or a more brutal ethnic naturalist view of race, it remained a practice predicated upon inequality. To be a member of what were variously termed 'backward peoples' or 'dependent nations' was to be denied the right to self-determination on the basis of racial classification. As we shall see later on in the chapter, it is precisely this hierarchical view of humankind which the minority rights response to race aims to prevent.

Race and multiculturalism

Since the mid-1960s, race thinking has largely fallen into disrepute within western democracies. Mainstream political parties and their leaders no longer invoke racial ideas in support of their domestic or foreign policies and instead are usually keen to disassociate themselves from those who do. This movement away from race-thinking is apparent in multicultural programmes and policies. Multiculturalism combines a rejection of externally imposed categories such as race with a recognition of voluntarily affirmed national, ethnic, religious or linguistic identities and associations. Those who aspire towards a multicultural community disavow racial hierarchy in favour of equality. Multicultural efforts to reverse the legacy of race-thinking have proceeded in two distinct albeit related directions – equality of treatment and equality of opportunity.

The principle of equality of treatment insists that individuals should be dealt with according to their own merits and not as a result of ascriptive characteristics such as race, religion and national or ethnic origin. Accordingly, conduct which discriminates on the basis of race, religion or national or ethnic origin is prohibited. Such requirements usually apply to all public institutions, agencies and officials, including, among others, the police, the military, courts, educational institutions and social services. They may also extend to private institutions or actors in the interest of an overriding public good such as commerce. For example, article II of the 1964 US Civil Rights Act guarantees 'full and equal enjoyment of the goods, services, facilities, privileges, advantages, and accommodations of any place of public accommodation . . . without discrimination or segregation on the ground of race, color, religion, or national origin'. A 'place of public accommodation' within the meaning of the Act is any establishment whose operations affect commerce or are supported by state action. A similar rationale underscores the European Union's 2000 Race Equality Directive which also applies to both the public and private sectors.

The principle of equality of opportunity goes one step further in advocating that possibilities for achievement, as for example in education and employment, should be equal for all citizens regardless of their race, religion or national or ethnic origin. Already in the 1960s, American civil rights leaders insisted that 'there is little value in a Negro's obtaining the right to be admitted to hotels and restaurants if he has no cash in his pocket and no job' (Steinberg 2000: 69). Such convictions underscore policies of affirmative action intended to ameliorate social disadvantage resulting from past racism. These policies include membership in minority groups as a criteria in employment practices such as hiring and promotion and in academic admissions procedures.

Neither of these approaches is without its critics. The 'colour blind' response embodied in the principle of equal treatment has been challenged by indigenous peoples and their supporters for failing to distinguish between segregation and forcible assimilation. From this perspective, the application of equal treatment formulas to strike down autonomous – and thus separate – arrangements for indigenous peoples is wholly inappropriate.

> The point is not that Indians [which herein refers to the indigenous population of the Americas] do not need protection against racism. But whereas racism against blacks comes from the denial by whites that blacks are full members of the community, racism against Indians comes primarily from the denial by whites that Indians are distinct peoples with their own cultures and communities. (Kymlicka 1995: 60)

At the same time, affirmative action has been attacked for perpetuating racial categories and classifications. The advocates of the 'colour blind' response argue that using skin colour as a basis for economic or social decisions ignores the fundamental reason why racial discrimination is repugnant in the first place – because it judges individuals on the basis of factors beyond their control. Other critics claim that the original 1960s justification for racial preferences – as a temporary remedy for past injustices – no longer applies. Thus, for example, it has recently been suggested that racial preferences ought to be replaced with or supplemented by economic indicators in order to ensure that affirmative action recognizes the socially disadvantaged whatever their race (Kahlenberg 2000; Gutmann 2000).

The dilemmas raised by affirmative action have been a prominent feature of political debate over the past three decades. This is especially true in the United States where such provisions are often described as forms of 'reverse discrimination'. Such allegations have become the basis for legal challenges under the Fourteenth Amendment of the US Constitution which guarantees equal protection of the law. One of the earliest cases to do precisely this was *Regents of the University of California v. Bakke* in 1978. Allan Bakke was twice denied admission to the University of California Davis Medical School despite better grades and test scores than successful minority applicants. The opinion of the court was divided: five justices supported the University of California while four favoured Bakke. The eventual judgment found that using race as one factor in admissions was legal but that setting aside a fixed number of places for racial minorities was illegal.

Although a landmark decision, the Bakke ruling by no means resolved the controversy. In 1996, the US Fifth Circuit Court of Appeals in *Hopwood v. Texas* found preferences to be just as illegal as quotas. That same year California voters passed Proposition 209 which prohibits preferential treatment on the basis of race, sex, colour, ethnicity or national origin in the operation of public employment, contracting and education. Similar legislation was passed in Washington State in 1998 and in Florida in 2000. In 2003, the US Supreme Court once again considered the potential discriminatory effects of affirmative action in two cases concerning admissions policies at the University of Michigan. As in Bakke, the court was divided and their contradictory judgments would seem to reflect rather than resolve the deeply rooted divisions in American public opinion on this issue. In *Grutter v. Bollinger* the court ruled 5–4 in favour of the University of Michigan's law school admissions policies that considered race as one factor amongst many, but in *Gratz v. Bollinger* they voted 6–3 to overturn an undergraduate admissions programme at the same university that relied more explicitly on race through a points system (CNN 2003).

These controversies confirm the ongoing significance of racial diversity dilemmas within contemporary politics. Race continues to be a deeply emotive issue not least because problems of racial injustice persist. The circumstances surrounding the death of Stephen Lawrence in London are a tragic reminder of this fact. Nevertheless, the historic significance of multicultural efforts to abandon race-thinking should not be overlooked. For the better part of a century (roughly 1850–1945), racial theories were widely accepted and played a key role in the formulation of both domestic and international policies. What William Bain notes with respect to international trusteeship can be applied to the politics of this period more generally: 'No matter now self-evidently wrong such thinking appears to us now . . . the idea of race . . . furnished answers to questions great and small that were in its time no less authoritative than those furnished by religion or science' (Bain 2003: 178). Dominant paradigms are never easy to displace. Race-thinking did not simply disappear from mainstream politics of its own accord, it was pushed aside by a combination of changed circumstance and deliberate public policy. The more extreme ethnic naturalist discourse was brought into disrepute by the Holocaust and lost much of its previous persuasiveness as a result. From this point onwards, it was more or less relegated to the margins of political life. But the more moderate civic progressive discourse persisted as a credible voice in public policy debates well into the 1960s. As late as 1957, for example, Lord Hailey could plausibly describe relations between peoples within the British Empire as 'a procession . . . in which great distances separate the van from the rear guard' (Hailey 1957: 150).

The belief that material (as distinct from natural) differences between races justified differential treatment was rejected as a basis for public policy only through the concerted efforts of public actors and institutions in the United States, the United Kingdom and indeed elsewhere. In the United States, for example, the conviction endorsed in 1896 by *Plessy v. Ferguson* that laws permitting and even requiring racial separation do not imply inferiority persisted until it was explicitly discredited by the Supreme Court in their landmark 1954 decision on *Brown v. Board of Education.* Even then, the legacy of Jim Crow was not publicly disavowed until the 1964 Civil Rights Act formally guaranteed equal voting rights and prohibited racial segregation or discrimination. In many parts of the south, these guarantees only came into effect through the direct involvement of federal law enforcement agencies acting against the wishes of state governors and legislatures and a majority of 'white' public opinion.

Similarly, proposals for legislation to prohibit racial discrimination in the United Kingdom met with stiff opposition during the late 1960s. In what has become known as the 'Rivers of Blood' speech, Conservative MP Enoch Powell claimed those who were in favour of legislation against racial discrimination had 'got it exactly and diametrically wrong'.

> The discrimination and the deprivation, the sense of alarm and of resentment, lies not with the immigrant population but with those among whom they have come and are still coming. This is why to enact legislation of the kind before Parliament at this moment is to risk throwing a match onto gunpowder. The kindest thing that can be said about those who propose and support it is that they know not what they do . . . As I look ahead, I am filled with foreboding; like the Roman, I seem to see 'the River Tiber foaming with much blood'. (Powell 1968)

Conservative leader Edward Heath condemned Powell as a 'racialist' and expelled him from the Shadow Cabinet. Nevertheless, Powell received over one hundred thousand letters in support of his position. Yet despite this public opposition, the United Kingdom's first comprehensive Race Relations Act was passed in 1968 (later to be superseded by the Race Relations Act of 1976).

Race between communities

Race as an organizing principle between communities performs a role analogous to race within community. Once again, the primary function of race is to determine which groups ought properly to exercise sovereign authority and which should be subject to the authority of another power. Here the key distinction is variously defined in terms of 'sovereign versus dependent nations' or 'civilized versus backward peoples'. In this usage, race parallels and thus discloses those characteristics deemed necessary for admission into international society and equal membership within it. Those deemed 'immature' for membership are accorded an inferior status within or in some cases even outside international society. Thus just as race is used to maintain a hierarchical system of inequality within communities, so it is used to support and justify a hierarchical system of inequality between communities.

Civilization and the 'white man's burden'

During the period of European hegemony over the non-European world – which lasted roughly from the middle of the nineteenth to the middle of the twentieth century – an international system of racial inequality was justified and perpetuated through a discourse on civilization. In this view, humanity was organized into distinct peoples who occupied different stages of civilization. A people's rights and responsibilities under international law were commensurate with their civilizational progress. Sovereignty was reserved for the most 'advanced', who in turn were expected to exercise a fiduciary responsibility over those deemed 'inferior'. Thus what Rudyard Kipling termed the 'white man's burden' became the justification for European imperialism.

The idea of a 'white man's burden' – although formulated in the discourse of civilization – was nevertheless imbued with the racialist thinking of the period, as the term itself makes clear. In both accounts, visible differences between peoples were understood and evaluated on the basis of European accounts of 'science', 'history' and 'progress'. These distinctions were then translated into a hierarchical political structure which located Europeans on the top, Asians in the middle and Africans and other tribal peoples at the bottom.

Europe and the non-European world The international discourse on civilization was a European response to the dilemma of non-European diversity. In contrast to the nineteenth century idea of race, the international society which emerged out of the previous Latin Christian universitas in Western Europe during the seventeenth century was predicated upon equality of interest and entitlement. At that time, international society was composed of sovereign princes linked by ties of marriage and descent who recognized one another as belonging to the same 'race of kings' and possessing a similar, divinely sanctioned authority over territories and populations. Equality in this context was a reflection of a shared history and common civilization which persisted into the new era of nation-states. Thus, well into the eighteenth century, Edmund Burke could plausibly speak of a 'Republic of Europe' to which all Europeans belonged regardless of ethnicity or citizenship. After the Congress of Vienna in 1815, this ideal of a European community beyond the level of the state found expression in the so-called 'Concert of Europe' system. Similarly, the standard of conduct between European states was representative of legal and philosophical traditions which transcended jurisdictional divisions. International law, for example, has its origins in the 'natural law' of the Latin Christian universitas and in the *jus gentium* of the Roman Empire. In other words, up until the nineteenth century international society was for all intents and purposes a European society not only in its membership but, more importantly, also in its underlying normative framework.

Once Europeans began to have sustained relations with diverse peoples in far-flung corners of the globe, this society was confronted with a serious dilemma: by what principles and practices should Europeans conduct their relations with the non-European world? Should non-Europeans be accorded the same rights as Europeans despite the obvious differences in race, religion, culture, political organization and technological development which existed between them? Or should international relations take note of and be commensurate with such distinctions? The answer provided by las Casas and Vitoria in the sixteenth century – namely that principles of Christian theology should govern such relations – was no longer convincing in the increasingly secular Europe of the nineteenth century. With religion unable to offer much guidance, a more 'scientific' approach was sought: in this context, the civic progressive view of history afforded a convenient solution.

On this basis, a 'scientific' concept of civilization was extrapolated from European experience. Civilization thus became a linear process which made it possible to think of peoples as occupying different points along a progressive scale and to make graded distinctions between them (Bain 2003: 100). According to this interpretation, what set Europeans (and especially West Europeans) apart from the rest of humankind was not religion or race per se but their material and moral achievements as disclosed in law, politics, economics, technology, education, culture and so forth. Such purportedly objective and observable facts made it entirely reasonable to privilege Europeans over comparatively 'less civilized' non-European peoples. By this sleight of hand, what began as a religious (Christian) and later culturally or geographically European standard of conduct was transformed into a secular organizing principle with global applicability (Gong 1984: 54).

The 'standard of civilization' The 'standard of civilization' became a convenient yardstick against which the 'progress' of humanity could be assessed. Peoples were hierarchically classified as 'civilized', 'barbarous' or 'savage' depending upon their degree of conformity with European practices and values (Gong 1984: 55). This classification scheme provided a basis on which to accord differential rights and entitlements within international relations. Such arrangements preserved the original principle of equality amongst European states while at the same time responding to those differences Europeans postulated between themselves and the rest of humanity.

The civilized sphere was in practice if not in principle restricted to Europe and European settler states such as the United States and the so called 'white dominions' of the British Empire (Canada, Australia, New Zealand and, paradoxically, South Africa). Only 'civilized states' were eligible for equal membership within international society and full protection by international law. Crucially, such admission into the 'family of civilized nations' was dependent upon 'approval' by existing members. This in effect gave the great powers of the day – all of whom were 'white' Europeans – a veto over the expansion of international society beyond the original West European core.

Purportedly 'barbarous countries' like the Ottoman Empire, China, Siam and Japan were understood to possess a 'kind of civilization', albeit of a non-European variety, but one as yet insufficient for the full satisfaction of international law. These 'semi-civilized' states thus found themselves in an anomalous position where they were expected to comply with some principles of international law but did not benefit from its full protection – hence they often became subject to 'unequal treaties' (such as in East Asia), capitulation (as with the Ottoman Empire), or protectorates (such as the British regime imposed on Egypt after 1884). Progress towards 'civilization' was in theory possible for 'barbarous peoples' but in practice this did not translate into full equality with Europeans. 'Like Sisyphus, the less "civilized" were doomed to work toward an equality which an elastic standard of "civilization" put forever beyond their reach. Even to attain a 'civilized' status, as Japan was to discover, was not necessarily to become equal. The "civilized" had a way of becoming more "civilized" still' (Gong 1984: 63).

Those peoples judged still within the 'savage sphere' were seen as bereft of civilization and as such 'lacked self-control, acted on passion, and knew only the satisfaction of will and appetite' (Bain 2003: 102). As Lord Lugard said of Africans, such peoples were akin to the 'child races of the world' and required 'civilized guardians and teachers' in order to 'progress' towards 'political maturity' (Lugard 1929: 69–72). Accordingly, it was entirely permissible under international law for 'civilized' states to acquire protectorate rights over such 'backward territories' (Lindley 1926). Because 'barbarous peoples' had no status in international society, international law did not apply directly to them and so those states exercising protectorates were answerable to their fellow members of international society and not the peoples they were purportedly 'protecting' (Gong 1984: 58).

The 'sacred trust of civilization'　As the nineteenth century progressed, it was increasingly assumed that those exercising protectorates were expected to comply with a 'sacred trust of civilization'. As defined in article VI of the General Act of the Conference of Berlin (1884) the European imperial powers agreed to 'bind themselves to watch over the preservation of the native tribes, and to care for the improvement of the conditions of their moral and material well-being and to help in suppressing slavery, and especially the Slave Trade . . .' Such convictions were institutionalized under the League of Nations Mandates System and the subsequent United Nations Trusteeship System. In each case, the rationale for these arrangements continued to be expressed in the discourse of civilization.

Article 22 of the League of Nations Covenant says with respect to those 'colonies and territories . . . not yet able to stand by themselves under the strenuous conditions of the modern world, there should be applied the principle that the well-being and development of such peoples form a sacred trust of civilization and that securities for the performance of this trust should be embodied in this Covenant'. The specific responsibilities required of each mandatory power as outlined in the series of mandate treaties roughly corresponded with the division of humanity into 'civilized', 'barbarian' and 'savage peoples': so-called 'A mandates' in the Levant were in the final process of development towards independence; 'B mandates' in tropical Africa were further removed from this goal and thus required a correspondingly more involved form of supervision; while 'C mandates' (which included South West Africa, New Guinea and Samoa) were at the 'bottom' of the 'civilizational' scale and thus in need of the greatest protection (Bain 2003: 100).

Similarly, article 73 of the United Nations Charter affirms 'the principle that the interests of the inhabitants of these territories are paramount', and requires states administering them to 'accept as a sacred trust the obligation to promote to the utmost, within the system of international peace and security . . . the well-being of the inhabitants of those territories'. Those states exercising fiduciary responsibilities over 'less developed' peoples were thus responsible for protecting them against abuse, guaranteeing their political, economic, social and educational advancement and guiding them towards eventual self-government.

The 'sacred trust of civilization' performed a role within international society analogous to the dual mandate within the British Empire. It was intended to limit the potential for European hegemony over non-European peoples to degenerate into blatant abuse and brutality. In practice, however, such international undertakings did little to constrain those European powers bent on the exploitation of non-European peoples and their territories. As E. D. Moral remarked of the Congo Free State, 'from the ashes of an international conference . . . has sprung a traffic in African misery more devilish than the old, more destructive, more permanently ruinous in cumulative effect' (Bain 2003: 70–1).

Even those who insisted that imperialism was more than simply a term of abuse had to admit that imperial powers expanded by force and in the process committed crimes against the local population (Perham 1967: 147). Colonial administrators often neglected their fiduciary responsibilities and the introduction of European 'civilization' undermined indigenous society while leaving little in its place (Perham 1967: 33–9). More fundamentally, the underlying belief in European racial superiority sustained stratified societies predicated on the fundamental inequality of peoples – and those Africans and Asians who challenged the 'progressivist' assumptions of civilization by demanding the same treatment as 'white' Europeans were invariably condemned as 'extremists' (Bain 2003: 132).

Equality of peoples

Against the hierarchical view of humankind organized into peoples, races or civilizations distinguished by their biological fitness or material and moral development stands the conviction that all humans are created equal and ought therefore to be treated as such. This conviction has a long history in western political thought from Christian 'natural law' theologians such as las Casas and Vitoria, through to Machiavelli, Hobbes, Locke, Rousseau, Paine, Jefferson, Lincoln, Marx and Woodrow Wilson. And it found expression in the ideals of the American and French revolutions which introduced the principle of popular sovereignty into world affairs. Even if many of these sources were not explicitly concerned with the problem of race as such, their implications for race relations were nevertheless immense.

Hitherto 'subject' peoples invoked precisely this tradition of thought in their bid to throw off the shackles of European 'tutelage' and 'protection'. In other words, Africans and Asians asserted their claims for political equality by holding the 'white' colonial powers accountable to their own standards (Bain 2003: 138). They were not alone in this endeavour; significant voices of dissent within the West also challenged ideas of civilization and racial superiority. Writers such as Richard Cobden, John Hobson, G. Lowes Dickinson, and Leonard Woolf directly attacked the justification for empire. They argued that the 'standard of civilization' was nothing more than a 'European conceit bearing no relation to reality': accordingly, there was no 'scale' against which 'progress' could be measured and therefore no reasonable basis for discrimination between peoples (Vincent 1992: 249).

Nor were these criticisms confined to intellectual debates; after 1945 they were increasingly voiced within the corridors of power on both sides of the Atlantic. In the United States Congress, for example, Wendell Wilkie insisted that 'there is no more place for imperialism within our own society than in the society of nations. The big house on the hill surrounded by mud huts has lost its awesome charm' (Bain 2003: 112). Similarly, in the British House of Commons, Tony Benn noted that the origin of so-called African extremist demands for political equality was to be found in British universities and in the British Parliament itself: 'here in this Chamber is the greatest revolutionary inspiration of the lot . . . if we can do it, why cannot they do it?' (Bain 2003: 138)

Two international developments were critical in shifting the burden of proof in this debate from the 'equal rights extremists' to the defenders of the 'white man's burden'. The preponderance of two avowedly anti-colonial powers, the United States and the Soviet Union – even if their anti-colonialism did not necessarily originate in a belief in racial equality – gave new impetus to decolonization debates (Vincent 1992: 252). The horrors of the Holocaust in Nazi Europe not only discredited the ethnic naturalist view of race but also made European claims to 'civilizational superiority' more difficult to sustain (Gong 1984: 87). Ultimately, the 'white' advocates of racial hierarchy were unable to respond in any meaningful way to the proponents of equality because they could not claim the

'Rights of Man' for themselves and at the same time withhold them from the peoples of Africa and Asia (Bain 2003: 139).

The expansion of international society before 1945   The entry of non-European peoples into the society of states began well before 1945. Between 1770 and 1820, there were a series of independence movements which ultimately resulted in the recognition of new states out of previous colonial possessions. However, these developments were confined to the Americas and resulted from secessionist demands by European settlers (Watson 1992: 127). Accordingly, they were relatively unproblematic in the context of prevailing views of racial and civilizational hierarchy.

The first truly non-European peoples to achieve political independence were the citizens of Haiti, Liberia and Sierra Leone – all of whom took as their raison d'être the ideals of the French Revolution. In Haiti, independence was won through an armed slave uprising against the French and finally declared by General Jean Jacques Dessalines in 1804. The words of Dessalines' proclamation are a clear rejection of European pretensions to superior civilization and an affirmation of freedom and equality:

> We dared to be free, let us dare to be so by ourselves and for ourselves, let us emulate the growing child: his own weight breaks the edge that has become useless and hamper[s] its walk. What nation has fought for us? What nation would like to harvest the fruits of our labors? And what dishonorable absurdity then to vanquish and be slaves. Slaves! Leave it to the French this qualifying epithet: they have vanquished to cease to be free. Let us walk on other footprints; let us imitate these nations whom, carrying their solicitude until they arrive on a prospect, and dreading to leave to posterity the example of cowardliness, have preferred to be exterminated rather than to be crossed out from the number of free peoples. (Dessalines 1804)

The Haitians took for themselves what the French were not prepared to concede to others: popular sovereignty.

In contrast, Liberia and Sierra Leone are a consequence of 'white' anti-slavery movements in Europe and North America. Nevertheless, the principle of equality was paramount for both the European abolitionists and the freed slaves who returned to Africa as a result of their efforts. Liberia quickly established a qualified kind of independence (remaining a de facto dependency of the United States) with a view to 'provide a home for the dispersed children of Africa' (Vincent 1992: 243). Sierra Leone, however, retained the formal and legal status of a British colonial dependency until 1961. Nevertheless, as a result of these early political developments, 'French revolutionary ideas about national self-determination were given a racial aspect that was to become a battle cry of new African states at the United Nations a century and a half later' (Vincent 1992: 244): the 'rights of men and nations' belonged to all humankind regardless of race, creed or colour.

Between 1856 and 1939, a growing number of non-European states gained admission into international society as evidenced by their accession to leading international treaties such as the Hague Conventions and the Covenant of the League of Nations: by the outbreak of World War II (in addition to Haiti and Liberia) these included Turkey, Japan, Siam, China, Persia, Iraq, Afghanistan, Egypt and Ethiopia. However, unlike the earlier examples, these cases are very much in keeping with the hierarchical principle of civilization: such states gained admission to international society only by demonstrating a reasonable conformity with European standards.

Japan's acceptance of European practices after the Meiji Restoration in 1868 is a telling example: territorial clans were abolished in 1871; a prefectural system was established in 1872; western-style educational and tax systems were introduced in 1873; and by 1912, Japan possessed a centralized, bureaucratic government, a constitution establishing an elected parliament, a well-developed transport and communication system, a growing industrial sector and a powerful army and navy which had successfully won two major wars (one of them against a major European power, Russia). Westernization was also apparent in changing social customs as disclosed by the popularity of European hats, jackets, trousers and shoes over traditional Japanese dress, and the growing interest in European politics, philosophy, literature, art, architecture and music (Gong 1984: 186–7). But this sort of 'civilizational progress' came at a price:

To become modern, if you are not a Westerner, means approximating to *Western* norms, adopting other people's values. For us [Westerners] the difference between modern and traditional is a difference between our own present and our own past. To Japanese [and other non-European peoples] the difference is one between *our* present and *their* past. Tradition is Japanese. Modernity is alien, imported. More than any Western country, Japan has two cultures; and reconciling them is one of the great problems of social and political stability. (Beasley 1980: 5–6)

Moreover, full political equality with western states remained elusive despite these impressive political, economic and military achievements. Although extraterritoriality (in which Europeans were exempt from local laws) ceased to apply in Japan in 1899 and despite the fact that Japan attended both the 1899 and 1907 Hague Conferences alongside the other 'civilized' states of the world, Japanese immigrants to the United States continued to be discriminated against. Indeed, the US Immigrant Act of 1924 was deliberately anti-Oriental and especially anti-Japanese (Gong, 1984: 199). Even more revealingly, Japan's proposal to insert a race equality clause in the League of Nations Covenant was blatantly rejected by the great powers. As Harold Nicolson records in his account of the Paris Peace Conference of 1919:

Mr Wilson then found himself in a grave difficulty. On the one hand the Equality of Man, as enshrined in the Covenant, implied the equality of the yellow man with the white man, might even imply the terrific theory of the equality of the white man with the black man. On the other hand no American Senate would ever dream of ratifying any Covenant which enshrined so dangerous a principle. On that occasion, the President had, by the skin of his teeth, been rescued by Mr Hughes of Australia. The latter insisted that no such nonsensical theory as the equality of races should figure in the Covenant. Lord Cecil was instructed by the British Empire Delegation to support Mr Hughes' contention in the League Committee. The Japanese, however, were not prepared to allow Mr Wilson this providential alibi. They put the matter to a vote. They gained their point by eleven votes to six. Mr Wilson, as chairman, was faced with the unpleasant necessity of having to decree that the Japanese amendment had 'not been approved' since it had failed to secure 'unanimous approval'. That incident had left even him with an uneasy feeling inside. (Nicolson 1945: 119)

International relations remained hierarchically structured according to civilization and race throughout the interwar period, notwithstanding the admission of non-European members. Indeed, such admissions are best understood as the exceptions which proved the civilizational rule – i.e., states which were judged according to European standards and found to have 'progressed' satisfactorily. The majority of 'backward peoples' remained precisely that in European opinion and were treated accordingly.

Decolonization after 1945 In the period since 1945, international society has expanded rapidly to include approximately 200 states, the majority of whom are non-European. These developments are in large measure a consequence of the decolonization of Africa and Asia, which is, in turn, representative of a deeper normative transformation within international society. The hierarchical standard of civilization which helped perpetuate European hegemony over non-European peoples has been replaced with a new principle of equality. This change is already apparent in the Charter of the United Nations (1945) which, unlike the Covenant of the League of Nations, contains an explicit endorsement of racial equality: article 1 identifies the 'purposes of the United Nations' to include the development of 'friendly relations among nations based on respect for the principle of equal rights and self-determination of peoples' and the promotion of 'respect for human rights and for fundamental freedoms for all without distinction as to race, sex, language or religion'.

As the subsequent UN Declaration on the Granting of Independence to Colonial Countries and Peoples (1960) makes clear, the implications of this new principle of equality are nothing short of revolutionary. The 'subjection of peoples to alien rule, domination and exploitation in all its forms' was not only illegitimate but 'contrary to the Charter of the United Nations' and an 'impediment to world peace': all peoples have the right to self-determination and thus are 'free to determine their own political status' and 'pursue their own economic, social and cultural development as they see fit'; 'inadequacy of political, economic, social or educational preparedness should never serve as a pretext for delaying independence'; instead, 'immediate steps' should be taken in all non-self-governing territories to 'transfer all powers to the peoples of those territories' 'without any conditions or reservations' and 'without any distinction as to race, creed or colour'. In other words, there would be no more 'standards of civilization' and thus no reasonable basis on which to delay the recognition of independence for non-European peoples. By the late 1960s, it 'no longer made sense to speak of a hierarchical world order in which a measure of development or a test of fitness determined membership in the society of states' (Bain 2003: 135).

International protection against racism

At the same time, international society became increasingly concerned with the problem of racism and those measures necessary to overcome it. The most egregious consequences of racism – murder and enslavement – were prohibited under the Convention on the Prevention and Punishment of the Crime of Genocide (1948) and the Supplemental Convention on the Abolition of Slavery and the Slave Trade (1956). Genocide includes actions committed with intent to destroy, in whole or in part, a national, ethnic, racial or religious group, including killing, causing serious bodily or mental harm, deliberately inflicting conditions of life calculated to bring about destruction of the group in whole or in part, imposing measures to prevent births, or forcibly transferring children to another group. Slavery and the slave trade refer to the capture, acquisition or disposal of a person with intent to reduce him to slavery; all acts involved in the acquisition of a slave with a view to selling or exchanging him; all acts of disposal by sale or exchange of a person acquired with a view to being sold or exchanged; and, in general, every act of trade in or transport of slaves by whatever means of conveyance. Both genocide and slavery now have the status of 'crimes against humanity' under international law.

Following on from these developments, the 1963 UN Declaration on the Elimination of All Forms of Racial Discrimination condemned discrimination as a violation of human rights, an obstacle to friendly and peaceful relations among nations and as a fact capable of disturbing peace and security among peoples. It called on states to take positive measures to combat racial discrimination and to promote tolerance and understanding between different nations and racial groups. The subsequent International Convention on the Elimination of All Forms of Racial Discrimination (1966) made provisions against racial discrimination legally binding on signatory states and established a UN committee to monitor state compliance with these undertakings. Under this convention, states are required to condemn racial discrimination and undertake without delay policies to combat it, including where appropriate special measures for the advancement of previously disadvantaged groups.

In addition to these specific instruments, protection against racial discrimination can be found in all the leading international human rights documents. Article 1 of the Universal Declaration of Human Rights (1948) affirms that 'all human beings are born free and equal in dignity and rights'. Article 2 goes on to stipulate that 'everyone is entitled to all the rights and freedoms set forth in this Declaration, without distinction of any kind, such as race, colour, sex, language, religion, political or other opinion, national or social origin, property, birth or other status'. Similarly, article 26 of the International Covenant on Civil and Political Rights (1966) stipulates that

> all persons are equal before the law and are entitled without any discrimination to the equal protection of the law. In this respect, the law shall prohibit any discrimination and guarantee to all persons equal and effective protection against discrimination on any ground such as race, colour, sex, language, religion, political or other opinion, national or social origin, property, birth or other status.

Provisions like these may also be found in regional human rights texts including article 14 of the European Convention on Human Rights, article 24 of the American Convention on Human Rights, and article 3 of the African Charter on Human and Peoples' Rights.

Such guarantees underscore the extent to which the principle of equality has become a fundamental component of international society. This point is perhaps nowhere more clearly expressed than in the international opposition to apartheid rule in South Africa. The International Convention on the Suppression and Punishment of the Crime of Apartheid (1973) defined apartheid and similar policies and practices of racial segregation and discrimination as 'crimes against humanity' and as such were contrary to the principles of the UN Charter and constituted a 'serious threat to international peace and security'. Subsequent economic sanctions against South Africa severely affected the South African economy and encouraged internal protest movements. At the same time, political, economic and military pressure was applied by the independent states of Sub-Saharan Africa. As a result of these various concerted actions, many apartheid laws – such as those prohibiting interracial marriages and requiring the segregation of public amenities – were repealed or fell into disuse by 1990. In 1991, President F. W. de Klerk abolished the remaining apartheid laws and called for the drafting of a new constitution. In 1993, a multiracial, multiparty transitional government was approved and in 1994 the African National Congress came to power in a racially free and fair election.

In a legal or procedural sense, all states and the peoples they represent are now equal. Nevertheless, substantive differences in wealth, infrastructure, public order, life expectancy and other indicators of political stability persist. Indeed, some states are so completely lacking in the basic provision of government for their citizens that they are often referred to as 'quasi' or even 'failed' states (as is the case, for example, with Liberia, Sudan and the Congo). It is also true that the majority of the world's richest states are to be found in Europe and North America, while the majority of the world's poorest states are to be found in Sub-Saharan Africa.

These facts have led some commentators to suggest that while the struggle for racial equality may have been won domestically in the victory over European imperialism, it continues in the world economic system (Mazrui 1977). What, if anything, ought to be done to address this inequality of opportunity remains controversial. For example, the Jubilee Debt Campaign based in London is lobbying for a world in which the people of the poorest countries are liberated from the crushing burden of debt, and in which the future financial arrangements between rich and poor nations are founded on fairness, accountability and transparency. While, in a slightly different approach, some of the participants at the Third United Nations World Conference against Racism in 2001 have suggested that western countries should pay reparations to those states that suffered from slavery and colonialism, including the descendants of slaves in the Americas.

In sum, race related issues remain a potent source of diversity dilemmas between communities just as they do within communities. Nevertheless, these problems – although serious – do not diminish the historic significance of the transition away from hierarchy and towards equality within international relations. A great deal has changed with respect to racial equality even if a great deal remains to be accomplished.

The rights of racial minorities

The 'problem of racial minorities'

Racial hierarchies categorize individuals, and by extension groups, on the basis of ascriptive characteristics such as skin pigmentation, stature and body shape. In this sense, race implies an external classifier of some kind who determines what the type and degree of racial resemblance is between individuals. Consequently, race – in contrast to religion, language or ethnicity – is in the first instance objectively imposed rather than subjectively affirmed. Race is primarily about the way other people see us and not necessarily the way we see ourselves. Accordingly, there is always the potential for either racial inclusion or exclusion against the will of the individual. When applied to politics, racial categories are used to distinguish ruler from ruled. Those individuals assigned to 'inferior' races are excluded from full participation in social, political and economic life. Instead of being 'masters of their own fate' they are subject to the political whims of others.

As this chapter has demonstrated, racial exclusion may operate both within and between communities. Moreover, those groups assigned a 'subject' or 'dependent' political status may not constitute numeric minorities. Indeed, in colonial circumstances, the reverse is more likely to be the case such that a majority native population of purportedly 'inferior' race is ruled by a much smaller 'white' colonial or settler elite. Such was the case in those European overseas empires which flourished from the middle of the nineteenth to the middle of the twentieth centuries. Similar circumstances prevailed in apartheid South Africa until the early 1990s.

But regardless of their numeric standing within the population, all those deemed racially 'inferior' share a non-dominant political status: they are excluded from full participation in social, economic and political life purely on the basis of ascriptive characteristics beyond their control. The 'problem of racial minorities' is thus an imposition of diversity against the will of the individual in order to perpetuate a hierarchical social and political structure.

The minority rights response

The minority rights response to racial diversity dilemmas is concerned with the elimination of externally dictated impediments to full political, economic and social participation. From this perspective, public policies aimed at the preservation of normative distinctions between individuals and groups on the basis of race are viewed as fundamentally illegitimate because they are unsolicited by the individuals so affected. There is a categorical distinction between diversity that is subjectively affirmed and diversity that is objectively imposed. Whereas the former is essential for the realization of individual and collective freedom, the latter is a denial of freedom. The language of race and racial hierarchy powerfully discloses this point; 'inferior races' are 'subject peoples' or 'dependent nations'; they require 'tutelage' and 'protection'; in Lord Lugard's words, they are 'childlike' and therefore incapable of managing their own affairs. In contrast, 'superior races' are 'master races' destined to rule over those deemed 'inferior races'. This category distinction explains why the minority rights response to racial diversity is qualitatively distinct from the minority rights response to religious, linguistic or ethnic diversity: those deemed 'racially inferior' do not want to preserve or promote the ascriptive differences which have been used as a pretext for their oppression – they want emancipation from them. For this reason, the category race is deliberately absent from those minority rights standard-setting documents which are directed at the preservation and promotion of diversity, such as the UN Declaration on the Rights of Minorities.

The right to self-determination

The core normative content of the idea of self-determination is that all adult men and women have the right to govern their own lives both individually and collectively. As article 1 of the International Covenant on Civil and Political Rights makes clear, 'By virtue of that right they freely determine their political status and freely pursue their economic, social and cultural development.' No people should be subject to external rule whether by a foreign power or by a particular group within the state.

Because racial categories have historically been used to deny full and effective political participation to those deemed 'inferior', the right to self-determination is an essential feature of the minority rights response to race. Often, self-determination is achieved through the reform of racially biased electoral systems. For example, the 1965 Voting Rights Act (which prohibited voter registration requirements, literacy tests and other practices that had effectively disenfranchised African Americans in the southern United States) was a key component of the American civil rights programme. Similarly, electoral reforms were also integral to the end of apartheid rule in South Africa during the early 1990s. In other situations, self-determination may involve the creation of new states, as was the case with respect to decolonization in Africa and Asia. But regardless of how it is achieved, the principle of self-determination ensures that all human beings are 'masters of their own fate' and not 'servants' to another.

The right to be treated equally

Racial hierarchies are fundamentally concerned with the creation and perpetuation of inequality. Accordingly, the right to be treated equally is an obvious and essential response to such circumstances. To be equal is to have the same rights and status. The principle of equality thus denies any claims to biological or moral superiority of one human being over another. Instead, article 1 of the Universal Declaration of Human Rights affirms: 'All humans are born free and equal in dignity and rights. They are endowed with reason and conscience and should act towards one another in a spirit of brotherhood.' From this perspective, racial discrimination is an offence against human dignity and ought properly to be prohibited. All individuals regardless of race should have the same access to citizenship, education, employment, occupation, housing and public amenities. According to the minority rights response, states should take effective measures to revise public policies and to rescind laws and regulations which have the effect of creating and perpetuating racial discrimination. They should also pass legislation prohibiting such discrimination and implement policies to combat those prejudices which lead to racial discrimination.

The right to be compensated for past injustices

More controversially, in some circumstances racial minorities may be considered to have the right to be compensated for past injustices. Such compensation may take the form of affirmative action programmes designed to ensure members of socially disadvantaged minorities have equal opportunities in education and employment. However, it is generally assumed in accordance with article 4 of the UN Convention on the Elimination of All Forms of Racial Discrimination (1966) that such measures should not lead to the maintenance of separate rights for different racial groups and they should not be continued after the objectives for which they were taken have been achieved, i.e., once equality of opportunity has been realized. As the Bakke, Grutter and Gratz cases discussed earlier in the chapter reveal, determining when these conditions have been realized is fraught with difficulty and thus likely to be very contentious.

Alternatively, compensation may take the form of financial reparations for the victims of slavery and colonialism, as was proposed at the Third United Nations World Conference against Racism (sometimes referred to as the 'Durban

Conference' after the city in which it was held) in 2001. But again, it is only to be expected that the details of such a plan, were one eventually to be agreed – which at present seems unlikely – would be difficult to implement. For example, which states should contribute to the fund, and in what proportions? Should those states which renounced slavery sooner pay comparatively less than those who persisted in the practice for somewhat longer? How should the monies be apportioned between the victims of slavery and the victims of colonialism and on what basis? Are the descendants of slaves in the United States and elsewhere worse off now than they otherwise would have been had their ancestors remained in Africa? If they are worse off, presumably we would need to know by how much since that is essential to fixing the level of compensation. But how exactly should such comparative disadvantage be calculated? Should rich African Americans be entitled to the same compensation as poor African Americans? Should either receive as much compensation as the poor of Africa whose plight is often much more desperate than even the most economically and socially disadvantaged Americans? These are only some of the issues that would have to be resolved before such measures could be adopted. Thus, the principle of compensation – unlike the principle of self-determination and equality – has not been universally recognized as an appropriate response to the problem of racial minorities.

Conclusion

As a political idea, race is about the hierarchical organization of humanity with a view to determining which groups are qualified to exercise sovereignty and which are better suited to a subject status. Race thinking became prominent in the period following the American and French revolutions when popular sovereignty emerged as the basis for political authority within states. With its emphasis on readily observable similarities and differences, race offered a convenient method by which to delineate one people from another. Civic progressives saw racial categories as indicative of differences in material and moral progress between civilizations; race thus became a pretext for policies of paternalism (including assimilation and political tutelage) directed at both 'colonial dependent nations' in Africa and Asia and 'internally dependent nations' in North America and Australia. Ethnic naturalists used racial criteria to identify organic communities in order to promote self-determination and protect against 'degeneration' due to racial admixture; race thus became a pretext for policies of exclusion (including segregation, anti-miscegenation, eugenics and in some cases even genocide) directed at racial minorities. Yet regardless of any differences in motivation or brutality, all racist policies judge individuals and, by extension, groups on the basis of ascriptive characteristics and prejudicial opinions beyond their control.

The minority rights response to race aims to prevent the imposition of normative distinctions between racial groups. In this context, the emphasis is on the promotion of equality rather than the preservation of diversity. In order to overcome the racist legacy of the past, the proponents of minority rights advance three distinct principles: self-determination; equality of treatment designed to ensure all individuals are treated the same regardless of race; and equality of opportunity designed to assist members of socially disadvantaged groups realize their full potential. Each of these programmes has at various times been subject to criticism and so race remains a potent source of controversy notwithstanding efforts to ameliorate this tendency.

4
Language

Introduction

Language may be defined as 'the method of human communication, either spoken or written, consisting of the use of words in an agreed way' (*OED* 1989). This definition immediately discloses the fundamental social context of language. To be a language, sounds, symbols, syntax and so forth must be agreed, that is to say they must be understood by more than one individual and so their usage requires a collective element. This explains why we tend to associate language with communities, as revealed in the second definition in the *Oxford English Dictionary* which refers to 'the language of a particular community or country' (*OED* 1989). This collective or communal aspect makes language a potential diversity dilemma.

Language as a diversity dilemma

For most of human history, the only language of political significance was that used by the ruler to conduct his official business (law, trade, diplomacy, etc.). In practice, this authoritative language was often limited to a small group of officials (such as scribes and courtiers). In such political circumstances, the everyday language spoken by men and women and the extent of linguistic diversity within the population was largely irrelevant. That is because authority came from above (the ruler, the divine) and not from below (the people). Utilitarian arguments might be made in favour of ensuring that the population, or at least a larger segment of it, understood the word – and thus the law – of the ruler. For such reasons, linguistic consolidation including the assimilation of minority languages began in England and France during the dynastic period. Nevertheless, the word of the ruler was law regardless of whether or not it reflected the speech of everyday life.

That fundamental assumption was challenged in 1848 when a new generation of revolutionaries sought to apply the principle of nationality in circumstances where pre-existing dynastic jurisdictions could not readily be transformed into popularly sovereign nation-states. In such situations, linguistic criteria afford a compelling and convenient answer to the question 'who are the people?' Mazzini, and others like him, resolved this dilemma by defining the nation as the 'universality of the citizens speaking the same tongue' (Namier 1963: 31). Once the nation is defined in this way, if existing political boundaries separate the members of linguistic communities then such boundaries are contrary to the principle of nationality and thus illegitimate.

This new emphasis on language as the determinant of nationality 'transformed it into what it had seldom been before, into a political issue for which men are ready to kill and exterminate each other' (Kedourie 1960: 70). It also had revolutionary consequences for the territorial status quo and, by extension, international peace and stability. Whereas previously the state and its inherited jurisdiction, laws and institutions had made the nation, henceforth the nation defined as a language community had the power to make and indeed to break the state.

Language within community

Language, and especially written language, is an essential part of human community because it is the medium through which norms are communicated. For this reason, there is an intimate connection between language and politics. Indeed, political life is largely conducted through the use of an authoritative vocabulary which identifies right and wrong conduct on the part of both ruler and ruled. Thus it is only to be expected that the form and content of the authoritative language is indicative of the mode of political community which it serves. In other words, the normative context not only defines the type of language used but also the motivation for and consequences of linguistic policies, including those directed at linguistic minorities.

Sacred language

Where political community is constructed in religious terms, the language of politics is also the language of faith – in other words, the authoritative language in this context is a sacred language. The medieval universitae of Latin Christianity and that of Islam are indicative of such circumstances. In each case, the sacred language is authoritative precisely because of its association with the divine order. Christianity is based upon the belief that the eternal Word (logos) 'became flesh and dwelt among us' (Oakley 1988: 154). Church Latin thus becomes the medium through which God's will is communicated to humankind. Similarly Arabic – as the language of the Qu'ran – was the embodiment of God's truth (Anderson 1995: 14).

Like the universitas whose authority it conveyed, these sacred languages were themselves universal. Throughout Latin Christendom and Islam the language of government and culture was Latin and Arabic respectively. These languages, and the communities they represented, recognized no limits to their authority and in principle at least aspired to a global inclusion. Within their territories, these sacred languages sustained a vertically organized community in which the educated elite could communicate regardless of their geographic or vernacular origins. Marc Bloch notes that in Western Europe during the medieval period Latin was more than simply the language of instruction; it was in fact the only language taught (Bloch 1961: 77). Thus the administrative elite throughout Europe at this time was from an early age trained to speak and write in Latin whatever their vernacular happened to be. We see evidence of this training in Peter Ackroyd's account of Thomas More's education in late fifteenth century England

(Ackroyd 1998: 15–49). As More's son-in-law later noted, young Thomas was 'brought up in the Latin tongue' (Ackroyd 1998: 18). At about the age of seven, More's education in Latin began at St Anthony's grammar school in London where the primary purpose was to teach Latin language and literature. Here, More and his fellow students were required to converse with each other in Latin. This emphasis on Latin as the medium for both instruction and conversation continued throughout More's early schooling and during his time at Canterbury College, Oxford. It was this training in Latin which equipped More for his subsequent role in public life and which provided the basis for his conversation with scholars, lawyers and diplomats throughout Europe regardless of any differences in their vernacular speech. The famous friendship between Thomas More and Erasmus, for example, was conducted entirely in Latin. The universality of Arabic in the medieval Islamic world was, if anything, even greater. In addition to the administrative elite, Arabic was also used as an effective means of general communication and, except at the lowest social levels, frequently supplanted local languages and dialects as the medium for commerce as well as culture (Lewis 1982: 71).

Where communal authority and membership are constructed in religious terms, linguistic diversity per se is largely irrelevant as a political issue. The mass population of Europe remained linguistically diverse in vernacular speech throughout the period of medieval Latin Christendom. In most circumstances, this linguistic diversity had little bearing on the official organization of Christendom, which continued to be conducted in the sacred and universalist Latin language amongst a small elite of clergy and other administrative officials. It is only on those rare moments when the mass population was mobilized for religious purposes that the extent of linguistic diversity and its potential threat to collective identity and membership is revealed.

The First Crusade offers a telling insight into later political dilemmas associated with linguistic differences. In November 1095, Pope Urban II addressed a large crowd gathered outside the Council of Claremont. Historians are not certain what language Urban spoke – although his origins were French – but evidently it was a language that the crowd could understand. Urban apparently emphasized the plight of Eastern Christians and the desecration of Christian holy places at the hands of the Muslim infidel and called for Christian volunteers to reclaim the Holy Land by means of war. The popular response to Urban II's call was immediate and overwhelming – probably far greater than had been anticipated. Moreover, it was not only knights who responded to his call but also a popular element from the lower ranks of feudal society (*Encyclopaedia Britannica* 2005a). Men from all over Western Europe landed on the coast of France 'speaking no recognisable language and only able to communicate their purpose by crossing their fingers in the sign of the cross' (Southern 1993: 20): thus began what is sometimes known as the 'People's Crusade'. This early attempt to organize a multilingual, polyglot military force foreshadows the dilemmas faced in later centuries when mass mobilization of this kind became a necessary part of political life. Interestingly, perhaps because of the logistical problems involved in such multilingual circumstances, subsequent crusades had a much narrower social basis and were therefore presumably more manageable in linguistic terms.

This European experience of linguistic diversity had no parallel in the Islamic context. Thus a fourteenth century Persian work on Europe emphasizes that 'the Franks speak twenty-five languages, and no people understands the language of any other. All they have in common is their calendar, script and numbers' (Lewis 1982: 71). As Bernard Lewis notes, this was a 'natural comment for a medieval Moslem accustomed to the linguistic unity of the Moslem world' (Lewis 1982: 71). Instead, the Muslim experience of linguistic diversity reflected religious cleavages and was most clearly revealed in the written word. Jews used the Hebrew script for Hebrew and for other languages that they spoke. Christians used the Syriac script for Arabic as well as Syrian. Muslims used only Arabic script. Both Persian and Turkish were written in the Arabic script and drew their intellectual and conceptual vocabulary almost entirely from Arabic sources (Lewis 1982: 72). Thus we see the assimilating influence of Arabic amongst Muslims in stark contrast to the linguistic separation of Jewish and Christian minorities. Such discrepancies paralleled the official status of religious minorities who for theocratic reasons were administratively segregated from the Islamic community of the faithful.

Dynastic language

The emergence of dynastic rule in Western Europe during the late medieval period marks the transition towards a vernacular authoritative language as distinct from the universalist sacred language of Latin Christendom. This change in linguistic practice corresponds with the growing political segmentation of Latin Christendom in the fifteenth and sixteenth centuries. European society continued to be organized along a hierarchical, feudal structure. But the supreme authority of the universalist pope and Holy Roman Emperor was increasingly usurped by an expanding group of princes and their dynastic families, who themselves claimed a divine right to rule such that political community began to fragment along dynastic lines.

Thus it is only to be expected that the language of the prince would begin to replace the language of the pope in the administration of dynastic possessions. The rationale behind this transition from Latin to the vernacular was a concern to bolster the power of the prince as distinct from that of pope and emperor. The choice of language was entirely utilitarian and intended solely for administrative purposes as language used 'by and for officialdoms for their own inner convenience' (Anderson 1991: 17). It did not reflect any desire to systematically impose the language of the prince on his subject population. For example, when Henry VIII administratively unified England and Wales 'his intention was not oppressive and did not constitute an attempt to eradicate Welsh nationality as such' (Macartney 1934: 41). Instead, it reflected a desire to secure effective control over those territories and populations which in dynastic terms were his legitimate, sovereign possession.

The preamble to Henry VIII's Act for Laws and Justice to be Administered in Wales in Like Form as it is in this Realm reveals Henry's dynastic (as distinct from the subsequent nationalist) logic:

> Albeit the Dominion Principality and Country of Wales justly and righteously is and ever hath been incorporated annexed united and subject to and under the Imperial Crown of this Realm, as a very Member and Joint of the same, whereof the King's most Royal Majesty of meer Droit, and every Right, is very Head King Lord and Ruler; . . . His Highness, therefore, of a singular real Love and Favour that he beareth his Subjects

of his said Dominion of Wales, minding and intending to reduce them to the perfect Order Notice and Knowledge of his Laws of this his Realm and utterly to extirp all and singular the sinister Usages and Customs differing from the same . . . hath ordained enacted and established, That his said Country or Dominion of Wales shall be, stand and continue for ever henceforth incorporated united and annexed to and with his Realm of England; and that all and singular Person and Persons, born or to be born in the said Principality Country or Dominion of Wales, shall enjoy and inherit all and singular Freedoms, Liberties, Rights, Privileges, and Laws within this his Realm, and other the King's Dominions, as other the King's subjects, naturally born within the same, have enjoy and inherit. (Macartney 1934: 40–1)

In this passage, it is clearly understood that Wales belongs to Henry, not to the Welsh. Nor does it belong to England, which in turn is also Henry's possession. Any rights or privileges which Henry's Welsh subjects enjoy originate from Henry and not from their membership in the Welsh nation. Henry's concern is to ensure that these Welsh subjects should know and abide by his laws, which Henry evidently considers to be the law of his dynastic realm and not of England or Wales per se. This rationale is consistent with the sixteenth century understanding of dynastic rule.

Dynastic authority was located in a divine right and not in any purported affinity between sovereign and subject. That is why it was entirely legitimate for territories and populations to transfer between sovereigns on the basis of marriage, inheritance, purchase, conquest, gift, etc., or indeed for a legitimate sovereign like Henry VIII to alter the administrative status of part of his dynastic possessions. From a dynastic perspective, the linguistic identity of the population had no bearing on the legitimacy of such decisions. Similarly, the motivation behind vernacular language policies was utilitarian rather than identity oriented.

This dynastic trend towards a sovereign vernacular was reinforced by the Protestant Reformation, which put a premium on bringing the word of God to the faithful and thus on printing and preaching in everyday speech. Protestant use of the vernacular in sermons and Bible translations encouraged the growth of a diversity of unified, literary languages in

Western Europe. After the 1648 Peace of Westphalia, religion was territorialized as the purview of each sovereign so that sovereigns determined the religious affiliation of their subjects. In this way, the Protestant and dynastic trends towards the vernacular converged and in so doing encouraged the growth of vernacular literacy beyond the administrative elite (Anderson 1991: 40). England under the Tudors is perhaps the classic case where religion and language combined to strengthen the power and authority of the ruling dynasty. The Church of England was originally created to serve the dynastic interest of Henry VIII and his desire for a male heir. Following on from this, use of the vernacular as the liturgical language was made mandatory by Henry's successors in two Acts of Conformity – one in 1549 under Henry's son, Edward VI, and the other in 1552 under Henry's daughter Elizabeth I. Such developments solidified both the relationship between church and dynasty and the daily use of the vernacular in public life.

Some scholars have suggested that this convergence between religion, language and dynastic authority created a political community and concomitant identity which was readily adaptable for subsequent national purposes (Anderson 1991; Schulze 1998). That may well be the case. However, it would be anachronistic to interpret the motivation behind these sixteenth century developments in the context of subsequent political ideas. Religious belief and dynastic ambition are qualitatively distinct from nationalist aspirations. In the sixteenth century, no connection had as yet been made between popular identity and political authority. This explains why Queen Elizabeth I actually reversed the homogenizing trend of her father's policy towards Wales. By authorizing the translation of the Bible and Book of Common Prayer into Welsh and by stipulating that the liturgy should be conducted in Welsh in all Welsh-speaking areas, Elizabeth gave a new impetus to the Welsh language and arguably laid the foundations for the modern national movement in Wales (Macartney 1934: 42). At the time, however, Elizabeth's actions are readily explained by her Protestant religious convictions: modern nationalist sentiment did not enter into her political calculations.

The same cannot be said for the linguistic policies of nineteenth century dynasts such as the Habsburgs and the Romanovs. In such cases, the dynastic principle was itself

increasingly anachronistic in the context of popular sovereignty and the principle of nationality. As a result, those
princes who continued to base their right to rule on dynastic
prescription faced a serious (if not impossible) political
dilemma – to accommodate themselves to nationalist political
thinking without undermining their own authority. This
attempt to graft a national identity on to the dynastic body
politic produced what Hugh Seton-Watson has termed 'official nationalisms', of which the Tsarist policy of linguistic
Russification is perhaps the best known example (Seton-
Watson 1977: 148). By the 1870s, policies of linguistic assimilation were underway in the ethnically diverse border areas of
the Habsburg and Romanov empires. Similarly, the Young
Turks endeavoured, with even less success, to impose turkifi-
cation within the multiethnic, polyglot Ottoman Empire. The
key distinction between the linguistic policies of Franz Joseph
(1830–1916) or Alexander III (1845–1894), on the one hand,
and Henry VIII (1491–1547), Louis XIV (1638–1715) or even
Joseph II (1741–1790), on the other, is that the former developed after and in response to linguistic nationalism whereas
the latter took place while the dynastic principle still prevailed.

Civic language

The emergence of popular sovereignty and representative
government towards the end of the eighteenth century gave a
new impetus to linguistic consolidation within states. Whereas the principle of dynastic sovereignty had located authority
firmly within the person of the prince (hence the famous
dictum of Louis XIV, 'L'état, c'est moi'), the new ideal of
popular sovereignty gave this power to the people such that
legitimate rule was constructed in terms of a popular
mandate. The state was no longer synonymous with the prince
but instead with the collective will ('we, the people'). From the
French Revolution onwards, language became a matter of
governmental concern precisely because it was through a
common language that the newly authoritative will of the
people could be expressed and communicated.

It was the firm opinion of the revolutionaries that all
Frenchmen were to speak French since it was assumed that this

common linguistic bond would reflect their unity and perpetuate their liberty. The Jacobin Barère, reporting to the Committee of Public Safety in 1794, called it 'treason to the Patrie to leave citizens in ignorance of the national language' and demanded that 'the language of a free people be one and the same' (Shafer 1955: 124). Various revolutionary policies and promulgations demonstrate this concern for linguistic unity as a precondition for national liberty. The National Convention of 1793–4 required all laws to be read to the people in French. In those districts where French was not the language of daily communication (as in Brittany), French language instructors were to be appointed to ensure that the law would be universally understood. In a similar vein, the Convention also decreed the establishment of publicly funded primary schools to teach French language and to train for the responsibilities of citizenship (Shafer 1955: 124–9). Although not immediately intended for linguistic purposes, the practice of universal military conscription introduced at this time also had a unifying linguistic effect. French was the language of command and thus military service unavoidably brought with it a certain degree of linguistic assimilation (Shafer 1955: 124).

Yet as Boyd Schafer points out, possibly the greatest stimulus to the use of a common French language during the revolutionary period was not the linguistic policies of the revolutionary authorities per se but rather the general change in the nature of government and the enlargement of its functions which occurred at this time.

> As more people participated in government, more had to understand what was being done on a national scale. As radical and new laws were rapidly promulgated, it became advantageous to understand them – for self-protection if for no other reason. As men entered the national services, civil and military, they found it necessary and expedient to understand and use the language of the law . . . (Shafer 1955: 124)

In other words, the new mode of representative government was not only conducted in the vernacular (as was much of dynastic government) but required the vernacular in order to engage with the people – and such engagement had of course become the basis for legitimate authority. The state was increasingly answerable to the people and vice versa through a publicly recognized language precisely because it was feared that without the existence of a common linguistic medium, public accountability would be impaired.

The central importance of a common, public language as a precondition for representative (or democratic) government is a recurring theme in liberal political thought and practice from the late eighteenth century onwards. The best known proponent of this view is John Stuart Mill whose oft quoted essay *On Representative Government* contends that 'among a people without fellow feeling, especially if they read and speak different languages, the united public opinion necessary to the working of representative government cannot exist' (Mill 1972: 361). Political stability in a democratic system of governance is thus often equated – indeed considered dependent upon – linguistic homogeneity. The obvious implication of this perspective is that linguistic minorities ought properly to be assimilated into the official, public language to ensure equal and effective political participation and the proper working of representative institutions. Linguistic diversity may, at best, be confined to the home but it should have no place in the public life of a democracy.

The Durham Report of 1839 is an early yet revealing example of this civic perspective on linguistic diversity. The report itself was commissioned by the British government following colonial rebellions in Upper and Lower Canada. It is famous as a seminal document of British imperial history since it recommended representative government within the Canadian colonies – and in so doing established the principle on which subsequent British colonial policy in North America and indeed elsewhere would be based. A fundamental component of Durham's proposal for self-government concerned the linguistic assimilation of the French (Quebecois) population of Lower Canada. Durham contends that

> a plan by which it is proposed to ensure the tranquil government of Lower Canada must include in itself the means of putting an end to the agitation of national disputes in the legislature, by settling, at once and for ever, the national character of the Province. I entertain no doubts as to the national character which must be given to Lower Canada; it must be that of the majority population of British America . . .
> (Coupland 1945: 150)

Lord Durham thus recommended:

> without effecting the change so rapidly or so roughly as to shock the feelings and trample on the welfare of the existing generation, it must henceforth be the first and steady purpose of the British Government to establish an English population, with English laws and language, in this Province, and to trust its government to none but a decidedly English Legislature. (Coupland 1945: 150)

A similar emphasis on linguistic assimilation as a key component of the creation and consolidation of civic institutions is a recurring theme in the state-building discourse from the mid-nineteenth century onwards. We see evidence of this rationale in the administration of mandated and trust territories, in the new or enlarged states of Central and Eastern Europe between the two world wars, in the decolonized states of Asia and Africa after 1945 and in the post-communist states of Central and Eastern Europe after 1989. In all of these cases, the logic underscoring policies of linguistic assimilation directed at minorities is strikingly similar to that outlined by Mill and Durham. The 1995 State Language Law of Slovakia is a typical example. It identifies the Slovak language as the 'expression of sovereignty of the Slovak Republic and the general means of communication for its citizens, which guarantees them freedom and equality in dignity and rights in the territory of the Slovak Republic' (Daftary and Gal 2003: 47). In sum, the logic of civic language parallels the logic of popular sovereignty; the people are presumed to be one and the public language of the state and its civic representative institutions is intended to embody this unity of political purpose.

Ethnic language

After 1848, the political discourse of civic language was augmented and in some instances overshadowed by a new emphasis on language as the embodiment of an organic, ethnic identity. Here the stress was not on the utility of a common language for the proper functioning of political institutions, but rather on the cultural significance of language as the natural and indeed essential medium through which each individual and, by extension, each community understood the world and their place in it. From this perspective, every language is a particular way of thinking. What is understood in one language can never be perceived in exactly the same way in another language; the essence of genuine, culturally specific meaning simply cannot be translated. Following on from this, true community is only possible amongst native speakers of the same original language since it is only in such linguistic circumstances that complete understanding and mutual sympathy can exist.

These linguistic arguments – which we can trace back to German romantic writers such as Herder and Fichte – gave a new dimension to the idea of popular sovereignty. If the only genuine communities were associations of original language speakers, then linguistic affinity was not simply a means to an end (the proper functioning of representative government) but an end in itself (the basis of popular sovereignty). Instead of being an expression of representative government, language was the basis of statehood. The nineteenth century quest for statehood thus became as much a philological as a political endeavour. Throughout the Habsburg and Ottoman empires in Central and Eastern Europe, local nascent nationalisms were expressed and developed through literary efforts: Adamantios Korais (1748–1833) helped invent modern Greek through his translation of the classics; Josef Jungmann (1773–1847) wrote a Czech grammer and history of Czech literature; Stephen Katona (1732–1811) wrote a history of Hungary; Dositej Obradovic (1739–1811) published in contemporary Serbian as distinct from old Slavonic; to name only a few examples (Kohn 1960: 527–76).

As Kedourie explains:

> it is incumbent on a nation worthy of the name to revive, develop and extend what is taken to be its original speech, even though it might be found only in remote villages, or had not been used for centuries, even though its resources are inadequate and its literature poor – for only such an original language will allow a nation to realise itself and attain its freedom. (Kedourie 1960: 67)

Consequently, linguistic diversity is problematic not in terms of institutional accountability or stability (as in the discourse of civic language) but because it confuses and potentially corrupts original language communities. Foreign accretions and borrowings obscure original meanings and in so doing threaten to weaken the mutual understanding and sympathy which is the special preserve of genuine community; accordingly such foreign intrusions must be 'cleansed' to preserve the purity of thought and concomitant identity. By the same token, in circumstances where one original speech community is assimilated into another, the former can have no experience of genuine individuality or community. In Fichte's words, such an assimilated language community is merely the 'echo of a voice already silent . . . they are, considered as a people, outside the original people, and to the latter they are strangers and foreigners' (Kedourie 1960: 68).

From this perspective, the only appropriate response to linguistic diversity is the creation of separate and indeed homogeneous political communities on the basis of linguistic affinity. Secession or irredentism thus become the obvious political objective of linguistic minorities. Meanwhile, the majority language community can tolerate or assimilate such minorities only at their own peril since either programme could potentially dilute the purity of their own linguistic usage. Such a conclusion, of course, unavoidably leaves those minorities who are incapable of forming their own, independent language communities vulnerable to policies of assimilation or segregation or expulsion or worse.

Imperial language

While the new politics of popular sovereignty was gathering momentum across Europe, a very different form of authoritative language prevailed in European overseas empires during the late nineteenth and early twentieth centuries. Here the normative justification for political authority resided in a so-called 'standard of civilization' which governed relations between 'advanced' and 'backward' peoples. Although this standard purported to be an objective basis for imperial government, it was unavoidably infused with European cultural assumptions, paradoxically including those inspired by prevailing European ideas about representative government and popular sovereignty. The 'enlightened' rationale for imperialism was the desire to bring European practices of good governance to non-European peoples, thus 'liberating them' from the tyranny of 'oriental despotism' or 'primitive savagery'. In its most objective characterization (as it came to be stipulated in international law and practice), 'civilized' (European) rule included the guarantee of basic liberties, an organized and efficient political bureaucracy, a western style domestic legal system and the maintenance of permanent avenues for diplomatic interchange and communication (Gong 1984: 14–15).

In order to fulfil these obligations, imperialism unavoidably involved the use of European languages within overseas territories. The provision of European style governmental administration overseas required a similar level of bureaucratic organization as that prevailing within the European metropoles, and this of course made imperial administration equally dependent upon a public language through which it could formulate and communicate law and policy. As a result, 'all the colonial peoples were brought into the modern world under the aegis of an imperialism which superimposed a European language on the native tongue' (Emerson 1962: 136). The language of imperialism was the language of the European metropole, its power and its functionaries. In many cases, it also served as a *lingua franca* between what was often an otherwise polyglot subject population within a colonial administrative unit (Emerson 1962: 136). But the imperial language was not the language of daily speech and it usually did not attempt to assimilate the general colonial population, presumably because the creation of a mass electorate along European lines was, for most of the colonial period, little more than a distant goal. Instead, imperial language assumed and indeed reinforced the practice of linguistic diversity within colonial jurisdictions.

The imperial language was the medium through which all interaction with European peoples – economic, political, military, religious, educational, etc. – took place. Imperial rule required the linguistic and indeed cultural assimilation of an indigenous elite capable of carrying out the daily administration of imperial affairs, precisely because a 'civilized government' along the lines specified above necessitated a commensurately 'civilized' bureaucracy. Europeans occupied the senior positions in the colonial service, but the remainder was staffed by an indigenous personnel. As a result, European overseas empires became dependent upon a native coterie educated according to 'civilized' European principles. To quote Thomas Babington Macaulay and his 1835 Minute on Education for India, imperialism demanded the creation of a 'class of persons, Indian in blood and colour but English in taste, in opinion, in morals and in intellect' (Anderson 1991: 91).

The linguistic arrangements of imperialism may thus broadly be compared to the linguistic practices of feudalism. A common language of government and education prevailed at the elite level but the rest of society remained characterized by linguistic diversity, and indeed was often linguistically fragmented into comparatively small language or dialectic communities. This linguistic practice is of course consistent with a form of political community in which authority was imposed from above and had little, if any, direct interaction with the majority population. Needless to say, such quasi-feudal practices could only be reconciled with prevailing European ideas about popular sovereignty and representative government by the claim that imperialism would, eventually, lead to self-governing jurisdictions on the European model. The European imperial elites tended to view this 'civilizing mission' as a long-term historical project, such that self-rule for subject peoples was in principle desirable but remained a distant goal in practice.

Yet ultimately, and indeed ironically, the political content of this purportedly civilizing discourse – which included not only a doctrine of good government but by implication also the ideals of popular sovereignty, political representation, and the doctrine of the Rights of Man – was itself the downfall of European imperialism. It was precisely the western educated indigenous elites who were fully conversant in the imperial language and its concomitant political ideas who took these western, civilizational beliefs to their logical conclusion – an immediate claim for independence on the basis of popular sovereignty.

> Since it was an age of nationalism in the West the achievement and maintenance of national unity and independence were central themes of the literature, history and political tradition to which they were exposed. . . . The academic fare which was

laid before them and the climate of ideas and expectations in which they came to live formulated for them their own grievances and aspirations and pointed the paths they might follow. (Emerson 1962: 199)

In other words, the discourse of popular sovereignty and representative government to which the indigenous colonial elites were exposed through their assimilation into the imperial language proved just as powerful and persuasive in Africa and Asia as it had already proved within Europe itself. In light of this new political thought, quasi-feudal assumptions were at best anachronistic and at worse abhorrent to the Enlightenment ideal of equal human dignity.

Multicultural language

All the modes of authoritative language surveyed thus far have tended either to ignore the existence of linguistic diversity as irrelevant for community constructed from above (sacred language, dynastic language and imperial language) or to problematize linguistic diversity as a threat to the order and stability of community constructed from below (civic language and ethnic language). There is, however, an alternative construction of community from below which recognizes linguistic diversity as constitutive of the state's positive engagement with its citizens: multiculturalism.

The multicultural discourse is, in this sense, an interesting amalgamation of the civic and ethnic linguistic traditions. While affirming linguistic particularism as an essential component of individual identity, it rejects the ethnic assumption that a variety of original languages cannot coexist within the jurisdiction of a state without jeopardizing individual and collective autonomy. At the same time, while affirming the desirability of an official civic language for public institutions and democratic dialogue, the multicultural discourse rejects the assumption that the state must necessarily be unilingual to ensure the proper functioning of representative institutions. Instead, the public space may be occupied by two or more officially recognized languages. Switzerland is perhaps the classic case in point. The Swiss Constitution adopted in 1874 and revised in 1998 recognizes no fewer than four official languages at the federal level – German, French, Italian and Romansch – while permitting the adoption of unilingual or multilingual policies at the cantonal level depending upon local circumstances and predilections.

In some cases, the multicultural discourse also rejects the civic assumption that a state should not act to support a variety of heritage languages within the private domain in case these might encroach upon or erode the public space of the official civic language(s). On this point, recent Canadian developments are instructive. The Canadian state is not only bilingual at the federal level (where both English and French are recognized as official languages) but also acts to preserve and promote a variety of heritage languages belonging to its various immigrant communities through Canadian Radio and Television Licensing provisions and voluntary language teaching programmes intended to ensure the survival of these immigrant speech communities. Such provisions are very much in keeping with the prevailing understanding of the rights of linguistic minorities, as will be discussed below.

It is worth noting that the United Nations Educational, Scientific and Cultural Organization (UNESCO) Management of Social Transformations Programme (MOST) Project on Linguistic Rights identifies 169 states with constitutional provisions for more than one language and only twenty-two with provisions for a single civic language. These facts would suggest that in so far as it is an officially acclaimed ideal (which may of course differ significantly from existing practice), the multicultural discourse has become the dominant linguistic paradigm in contemporary politics. Why this should be the case is not immediately apparent and indeed would seem to contradict much of nationalist thinking of both the civic and the ethnic variety. It may well be that the sheer extent of human linguistic diversity – according to the Endangered Language Repository, there are currently about 6,800 living languages – makes the recognition of more than one official language increasingly unavoidable in the context of a general conviction (premised on popular sovereignty) that the state ought to be able to communicate with its citizens.

Language between communities

The authoritative use of language is also a characteristic of relations between communities, where it is a feature of both society and autonomy. Mutual comprehension, whether of each other's authoritative language or indeed of a shared *lingua franca*, is necessary for relations between communities. Thus a concern for language, and by extension linguistic minorities, enters into international politics as a part of the mutual recognition and communication between distinct communities which is a precondition for the existence of international society. At the same time, however, differences in authoritative language – whether by cause or effect – are indicative of the jurisdictional boundaries between communities. As such, linguistic diversity is a powerful reminder of the pluralist structure of international society. Here too, however, it is the prevailing normative understanding of authority within a state which determines whether or not linguistic differences will become matters of significance in relations between states.

Silence between medieval universitae

Sustained international relations necessary for the emergence of an international society can only arise between communities in which the relevant political authorities are prepared to acknowledge one another as equally autonomous. Such acknowledgement is not as straightforward as it seems since it requires the acceptance of territorially limited jurisdiction. As previously discussed, no international society was possible between the medieval Latin Christian and Islamic universitae precisely because each aspired to universal rule.

The universalist normative framework of these two communities was apparent not only in their internal use of a sacred language to sustain a community of faith over an otherwise polyglot population but also in their inability to produce a sustained diplomatic dialogue with outsiders, particularly each other. Prior to the eleventh century, contact between the two universitae was limited at best. The crusades and especially the crusader states initiated a new structure of relations (commercial as well as military) between the Latin West and the Muslim

East. However, neither side viewed these exchanges in terms of equality. Moreover, social segregation continued to separate Christians from Muslims – both during and after the crusader states – and thus limited the possibility of direct linguistic contact and dialogue between them (Lewis 1982: 21–33).

In the Latin West, attempts to overcome this linguistic separation for the purposes of trade and later also diplomacy began relatively early. The first Latin–Arabic glossary was compiled as early as the twelfth century, although a Latin treatise on Arabic grammar did not appear until 1538 (by which time numerous other glossaries and dictionaries were circulating in the West) (Lewis 1982: 80). However, no comparable interest in the Latin language was forthcoming within the Muslim East.

There are several possible explanations for this difference in linguistic openness. Western Europe was characterized by a much more extensive diversity of everyday speech such that the practice of learning language for the purpose of commerce was already well established. At the same time, the growth of Arabic studies in the Latin West occurs at precisely that historical moment when the transition from Latin Christian *universitas* to international society of dynastic princes was underway, i.e., between the fifteenth and eighteenth centuries. No comparable developments towards linguistic openness existed in the Muslim East both because of the sacred language's greater penetration of everyday speech (including commercial activity) and because the religious significance of Arabic as the language of the Qu'ran – and thus literally the word of God – made it almost sacrilegious for a Muslim to learn an infidel language (Lewis 1982: 72). Arguably these circumstances reinforced the normative integrity of the Islamic *universitas* and in so doing forestalled movement towards an international society.

Interestingly, the Muslim failure to acquire foreign language skills meant that those Christian minorities who combined fluency in Arabic with some knowledge of a European language often played an intermediary role between East and West. Thus knowledge of foreign languages became a specialized skill belonging to certain non-Muslim communities (such as the Greeks of the Phanar district in Istanbul). In this sense, then, linguistic diversity was an asset to minority communities under Muslim rule. However, it must be remembered that these linguistic opportunities resulted from and thus did not change their inferior status as *dhimmis* or non-Muslim subjects of the Islamic universitas (Lewis 1982: 78). Thus linguistic specialization becomes yet another feature of the Muslim practice of religious segregation.

Dialogue within international society

A common authoritative language is essential for the proper functioning of an international society since shared norms and institutions must by definition be mutually intelligible to all members. In this sense, then, the role of authoritative language within international society is comparable to the role of authoritative language within a domestic community. In each case, language is the medium through which standards of right and wrong conduct are communicated.

However, such communication is comparatively more complicated between communities than it is within communities since at this level linguistic diversity is both a defining characteristic of the association (and its plural membership) while also a potential barrier to understanding. Although such inconsistencies between linguistic diversity and public accountability within states have historically been resolved by either linguistic assimilation or linguistic separation, neither solution is possible within the context of an international society. The preservation of its plural and by implication diverse membership is the central purpose of an international society and so assimilation would be anathema. At the same time, however, complete separation would result in the breakdown of international society as autonomous communities retreated within themselves leaving nothing but an anarchic void between them. As previously discussed, the art of translation is one way to resolve this dilemma but as the numbers of international society increase, this task becomes ever more difficult to achieve. For this reason, members of international society have often found it expedient to adopt a common authoritative language in which to conduct their international discourse. Such a language is generally referred to as a *lingua franca*.

A *lingua franca* bridges the linguistic divide which usually parallels jurisdictional boundaries. Latin was the *lingua franca* of the sixteenth and seventeenth centuries; French performed a similar function in the eighteenth and nineteenth centuries; and since the twentieth century English has emerged as the language of global communication. None of these languages is intended to displace the authoritative language of the various member states of international society but rather to coexist alongside them. Nevertheless, diversity dilemmas may and do arise in this context as the global language by its very prevalence begins to penetrate the various state languages. This explains the French government's attempts to halt and reverse the influence of English on French by prohibiting the use of 'franglais' words and inventing French equivalents for new concepts, technologies, etc.

Language and territory

For the most part, however, problems of linguistic diversity, including the status of linguistic minorities, enter into international society through a prior concern with territory. International society is a real estate model (Mayall 1990: 26). In other words, the members of international society are distinct communities as defined by their authoritative and exclusive control over territory and the population within it. Linguistic diversity is closely related – by cause and effect – to this territorial framework.

Territories defining languages When an international society began to emerge out of the previous Latin Christian *universitas* in the sixteenth and seventeenth century, language – like religion – was seen as the purview of the sovereign. The authoritative language employed within the territory of a dynastic state reflected the will of the prince and not that of his subject population. Even after the principle of popular sovereignty had replaced the divine right of kings as the source of governmental authority, civic states continued to view language as a function of jurisdiction. Thus, in both the dynastic and the civic state, territory defined language and not the other way around. For this reason, language was unlikely to enter into international relations. Even on those occasions where territory was transferred from one sovereign jurisdiction to another in which different authoritative languages prevailed, language was not identified as a matter of significance and no provisions were made for any linguistic minorities which may have been created by the territorial readjustments.

This failure to provide for linguistic differences contrasts sharply with the widespread practice of stipulating treaty guarantees for religious minorities in transferred territories. This is the case even where religious differences parallel linguistic distinctions. For example, the Treaty of Paris (1763) which transferred hitherto French territory in North America to the British crown made no provisions whatsoever for the use of French, although it did include guarantees for the free practice of the Catholic religion. These Catholic minorities were for the most part also francophone minorities, but only their religious (and not their linguistic) identity was a matter of international attention. Similar inconsistencies may be found in the 1815 Final Act of the Congress of Vienna.

Because language did not feature in either the dynastic or civic definition of legitimacy, linguistic affinity – or the lack of it – between the sovereign authority and the population it ruled clearly was not perceived as a threat to international order and stability. Language was the servant of the state and thus it was accepted practice that the authoritative language would trump all others within its jurisdiction. In such circumstances, minority languages could not threaten the internal stability or territorial integrity of a state. Similarly, neither dynasts nor civic nationalists could imagine linguistic affinity as a pretext for war, secession or irredentism.

Languages defining territories These assumptions were challenged by the ethnic nationalists for whom original language was the source of genuine community and thus the only 'natural' – and by implication just – basis on which to delineate frontiers between states. As Fichte notes:

> The first truly original and natural boundaries of a state are . . . beyond doubt the internal boundaries. Those who speak the same language are joined to each other by a multitude of invisible bonds by nature herself, long before any human art begins; they understand each other and have the power to make themselves understood more and more clearly; they belong together

and are by nature one and inseparable whole . . . From this internal boundary . . . the making of the external boundary by dwelling place results as a consequence; and in the natural view of things it is not because men dwell between certain mountains and rivers that they are a people, but, on the contrary, men dwell together . . . because they were a people already by a law of nature which is much higher. (Kedourie 1960: 69–70)

From this ethnic perspective, the relationship between language and territory is reversed. Instead of language being a consequence of territory, and in particular a territorially defined jurisdiction, territory is a consequence of linguistic affinity. For ethnic nationalists, language (as evidence of a pre-existing, organic community) should define the state. Such a conclusion had enormous implications for the territorial status quo in Europe and indeed elsewhere. Suddenly, all juridical divisions were suspect unless they could be justified on 'natural', usually linguistic grounds. This point is summed up by a character in Fichte's dialogue, *Patriotism and its Opposite*: 'The separation of Prussians from the rest of the Germans is purely artificial . . . The separation of the Germans from the other European nations is based on Nature. Through a common language and through common national characteristics which unite the Germans, they are separate from the others' (Kedourie 1960: 68).

Linguistic arguments of this kind began to feature in political plans to redraw the map of Europe from the mid-nineteenth century onwards. Such assumptions were of course well suited to the political problem of creating nation-states in the absence of inherited jurisdictions. This of course was the predicament facing would-be nationalists in Central, Southern and Eastern Europe where national communities could only be formed by rearranging (through unification or separation) the boundaries of dynastic states and empires. For this reason, territorial claims based on linguistic affinity feature prominently in the creation of Italy, Germany, Poland, Yugoslavia and Czechoslovakia. This emphasis on language as a legitimate means of delineating frontiers reached its apogee in 1919 when the Paris Peace Conference dispatched linguists and ethnographers across Central and Eastern Europe with a view to assisting the work of the so-called Committee on New States. However, as this committee was quick to discover, the actual pattern of linguistic usage was complex and highly variable, which made it a very imprecise tool in drawing borders. In other words, regardless of any arguments to the contrary, linguistic diversity could not be overcome through territorial redistribution and thus linguistic minorities remained in many of these new nation-states.

Minority language rights and territorial settlements

From this point onwards, provisions for linguistic minorities become a feature of multilateral and bilateral treaties – especially in those circumstances where the territorial status quo was implicated (as in the creation of new states or the resolution of boundary disputes between states). The recognition of new or enlarged states during the interwar period included fairly extensive provisions for linguistic minorities. The resulting League of Nations System of Minority Guarantees gave linguistic minorities the right to use their minority languages in private, in commerce, in religion, in the press and in public meetings. At the same time, linguistic minorities were also eligible for minority language education in certain circumstances (at the primary level and where numbers warranted) and could use their minority language either orally or in writing before the courts. Similar minority language provisions were included in those treaties which established League of Nations mandates over former Ottoman possessions in the Middle East (especially as regards Palestine, Lebanon and Syria) and in the recommendations of the United Nations Trusteeship Council which assumed responsibility for these mandated territories after World War II (as for example in the Statute for the Free City of Jerusalem).

After World War II, multilateral minority provisions were rejected in favour of bilateral arrangements. Here, too, the practice of according language rights to linguistic minorities in disputed boundary areas continued. The De Gasperi–Gruber Agreement of 1946 which settled the status of the disputed South Tyrol boundary region between Italy and Austria is an interesting case in point. The South Tyrol had been a part of the Habsburg Empire until it was ceded to Italy by the Treaty of St Germain in 1919. After the Fascists came to power in 1922, the Italian government began a policy of Italianization.

This culminated in 1939 with the so-called Option Agreement between Italy and Germany (which by then included Austria). Under the terms of this agreement, the German minority on the Italian side of the border could either opt to remain culturally and linguistically German – in which case they would be relocated to the German Reich – or stay in Italy and relinquish their German language and culture in favour of Italian. By the end of the year, 93 per cent of the German speaking population decided to leave Italy, but the process of resettlement was slow to begin and eventually postponed as a result of World War II. Consequently, a substantial German minority remained in Italy after 1945. Under the terms of the De Gasperi–Gruber Agreement, the Italian government agreed to provide primary and secondary education in German to members of this minority community and to ensure parity of German and Italian in the regional administration (Jackson Preece 1998b: 116).

Similar provisions for linguistic minorities in the disputed region of Schleswig-Holstein were concluded between Denmark and Germany in 1955 (Jackson Preece 1998b: 116). And the 1955 Austrian State Treaty – which ended Allied occupation and administration there – recognized Slovene and Croatian alongside German as official languages in the border areas of Carinthia, Burgenland and Styria (Jackson Preece 1998b: 116). Since 1989, language provisions for minorities in disputed territories have become recommended international practice as evidenced not only in the various minority rights standard-setting documents of the United Nations, OSCE and Council of Europe but also in a range of agreements aimed at resolving self-determination disputes, including the Northern Ireland Peace Agreement, the Constitutional Framework for Provisional Self-Government in Kosovo, the Framework Agreement for Macedonia, the Law on the Special Legal Status of Gagauz and the Mindanao Final Agreement (Jackson Preece 2003: 12).

Language and human rights

A concern for language also enters into international relations through the various human rights instruments recognized at the United Nations and in other regional organizations since

1945. Here language is significant because of its relationship to the universal principle of human dignity. But the emphasis is placed on freedom of expression per se and not the particular language in which such expression occurs. Thus, for example, article 19 of the Universal Declaration of Human Rights (1948) recognizes that 'everyone has the right to freedom of opinion and expression; this right includes freedom to hold opinions without interference and to seek, receive and impart information and ideas through any media and regardless of frontiers'. Similar guarantees may be found in article 10 of the European Convention on Human Rights, article 13 of the American Convention on Human Rights and, in a somewhat more abridged form, article 9 of the African Charter. This understanding of freedom of expression is consistent with the civic discourse of representative language out of which it emerges.

The earliest formulations of the right to freedom of expression originated in the context of developing practices of representative government. So, for example, the 1689 English Bill of Rights sought to protect freedom of expression within Parliament from undue restrictions by the sovereign (Sieghart 1986: 141). By the time the US Bill of Rights was added to the American Constitution in 1791, the principle of freedom of expression had become a right belonging to the now popularly sovereign people which even their representative institutions were expected to respect. Hence the famous First Amendment of the United States Constitution guarantees that 'Congress shall make no law . . . abridging the freedom of speech or of the press'.

More recently, a concern for freedom of expression has become a significant feature of international efforts to promote democratic government. For example, during the Cold War, western governments and indeed non-governmental organizations like Helsinki Watch sought to assist the dissident movement by calling on communist states to respect their international and domestic undertakings in the area of freedom of expression. Following on from this, an interest in freedom of expression has now become a fundamental component of international efforts to encourage democratization within states. But this interest has been overwhelmingly concerned with the substance of what people should be free to say.

Little, if any, attention has been paid to the issue of what language people should be able to freely express themselves in. This oversight suggests a concern first and foremost with the civic or authoritative language of state and not with minority languages. Here, it is perhaps important to note that policies of linguistic assimilation may be justified by the ideal of universal freedom of expression in the official language of state. Hence general human rights provisions for freedom of expression may be of limited use for those minority language speakers who wish to express themselves outside of the state language.

The rights of linguistic minorities

The 'problem' of linguistic minorities

As the previous discussion indicates, language is integral to any community because it is the medium through which norms are communicated. However, an authoritative language does more than simply express norms; it also embodies them. Authoritative language is emblematic of a particular conception of community, its territorial extent, who belongs to it, and where authority resides within it. This explains the potential for language to become a diversity dilemma, especially once legitimate rule requires a popular mandate. Unlike religion, language per se cannot be separated from the state and relegated to the private domain – at least one language must be publicly recognized and affirmed as authoritative. Where the institutions of government require a popular mandate, as in the context of a nation-state, the authoritative language must extend beyond the ruling elite to the public at large. Unavoidably, this requirement privileges the authoritative or officially recognized language, which, because it is the language of state (including government, the courts, the military and other state funded institutions such as national banks, schools, universities, radio and television stations, etc.), usually comes to dominate social life. In such circumstances, minority languages are largely relegated to the home and may, over time, as their social significance declines, disappear altogether, as in the case of French among Quebecois immigrants in New England.

Consequently a frequent outcome, intentional or otherwise, of official language policies is a gradual process of minority language assimilation. For example, it has been suggested that the Slovak Official Language Law of 1990 which purported to clarify the authoritative language of Slovakia was intended to restrict the use of minority languages even in regions where such languages predominated (Daftary and Gal 2003: 43). Similarly, authoritative language requirements included in the post-independence language laws of the Baltic states during the 1990s were widely viewed as attempts to linguistically segregate Russian-speakers (Jarve 2003: 82).

Linguistic assimilation may also take a more direct and potentially even violent form. In addition to supporting the authoritative language, public policies may specifically target minority languages and their speakers, for example, by prohibiting the use of minority language place names and personal names or by requiring otherwise private institutions (religious, educational, cultural, etc.) to use the authoritative language. Practices such as these were used by Todor Zhivkov's government in Bulgaria during its 1980s campaign to 'Bulgarize' the Turkish minority (Poulton 1991: 105–61). In this case, individuals were forced to adopt Bulgarian equivalents to Turkish personal names, often at gunpoint. Those who refused to assimilate lost their jobs, were denied access to education and faced possible imprisonment. Ultimately, these and other coercive measures directed at the Turkish community resulted in a mass refugee flow from Bulgaria to Turkey – thus demonstrating how domestic diversity dilemmas can affect relations between as well as within states.

The minority rights response

The minority rights response to linguistic diversity accepts the necessity for an authoritative language policy within states but insists that such policies need not preclude the preservation of minority languages. This unavoidably means that the rights of linguistic minorities must be balanced against the right of a state to safeguard its authoritative language. It is therefore generally accepted that a state may reasonably require its citizens to demonstrate a minimal fluency in the authoritative language. Similarly, it is also understood that some minority languages should be given priority over others. A distinction is therefore often made between languages which are traditionally used within the territory of a state and the imported languages of immigrants, migrants or refugees. For example, the United Kingdom recognizes Welsh, Gaelic, Irish and Ulster Scots as regional or minority languages under its obligations to the European Charter for Regional or Minority Languages. This list excludes Arabic, Cantonese, Hindi, Italian, Turkish or any of the other languages spoken by its immigrant, migrant or refugee minority communities which fall outside the Charter's 'traditionally used by nationals of the State' rubric.

Moreover, even amongst indigenous minority language speakers, further requirements are often introduced such that minority language guarantees only apply where sufficient numbers warrant or where it is traditionally used within a state. So, for example, the Austrian State Treaty of 1955 recognizes the rights of Croatian and Slovenian language speakers in Carinthia, Burgenland and Styria but not beyond these internal administrative boundaries (Jackson Preece 1998b: 116). By 2000, due to an influx of immigrants and refugees from former Yugoslavia, a significant Croatian language community could be found outside these specified enclaves but such Croatian speakers were not entitled to any language rights under the original 1955 provisions. In this case, geographic location and not linguistic usage per se determines who may reasonably claim minority language rights.

Thus the territorially defined state with its own distinct authoritative language practices provides the context in which minority language rights are construed and implemented. In so doing, provisions for minority language speakers are one response to the dilemmas raised by linguistic diversity within states but they do not remove the necessity of balancing between competing claimants (e.g., individuals versus groups, the authoritative language community versus the minority language community) and potentially contradictory principles (e.g., mutual comprehension versus linguistic expression).

The right to speak a minority language

The right to freedom of expression in the language of one's choice is central to the idea of minority language rights. From this perspective, language is more than a utilitarian medium of communication; it is representative of specific cultural values and identifications. If the primary value of language is simply to facilitate communication then we should all want to speak the language with the greatest number of speakers. In such circumstances, the logical expectation would be for minority language speakers to voluntarily choose to assimilate into the more widely understood authoritative language within the state and, increasingly, for the authoritative language within the state to converge with the authoritative language within international society. If this expectation were correct, then ultimately humanity would speak a single, global language. While it is true that English as the current *lingua franca* is acquiring ever more speakers around the world, fluency in the English language is not so much displacing state or indeed local languages but rather coexisting alongside them. Individuals tend to remain conversant in their native languages despite the utilitarian benefits to be gained from abandoning these in the interest of better communication with greater numbers of people. This fact would seem to suggest that the value we accord to language goes beyond mere communication. Instead, language becomes entangled in and indeed representative of a particular way of life. Minority language speakers thus want to do more than simply communicate their ideas or opinions; they want to express a particular ethnic, religious or cultural identity and the only way they can do that is to speak the traditional language associated with it. For this reason, minority language rights should be distinguished from the general right to freedom of expression.

Article 27 of the International Covenant on Civil and Political Rights stipulates that 'in those states in which . . . linguistic minorities exist, persons belonging to such minorities shall not be denied the right, in community with the other members of their group . . . to use their own language'. The significance of this provision and others like it (which can be found in the UN Declaration on the Rights of Minorities, the Framework Convention for the Protection of National

Minorities, the European Charter for Regional or Minority Languages and ILO Convention No. 169 Concerning Indigenous and Tribal Peoples in Independent Countries) originates in their recognition of the minorities' 'own language' and the right to freedom of expression in this particular medium as distinct from the authoritative language of the state. The right to speak is thus central to all minority language guarantees. The corresponding assumption is that states have a responsibility to ensure that such minority language expression is not impeded or infringed and that no discrimination results from it. Such guarantees are intended to protect against those situations where minority language speakers are directly or indirectly prevented from using their own language in private associations (religious, educational, social, commercial, etc.) and communications (letters, newspapers, books, recordings, etc.).

In certain circumstances, the private use of language may involve a public aspect. For example, an individual may choose to be identified by a minority language personal name or may speak a minority language in a public place or a private minority language sign or inscription may be visible to the public at large. However, the right to speak a minority language does not in and of itself impose any requirements upon the state to recognize the minority language as authoritative within public institutions or to permit minority language communication with public officials or even to provide translation services for those minority language speakers insufficiently fluent in the authoritative language. It is therefore not only the most basic but also the least controversial component of minority language provisions.

The right to state-funded education in a minority language

The right to a state-funded education in a minority language is potentially much more problematic with respect to the preservation of the state's linguistic monopoly over authoritative language. The basic right to speak a minority language includes the right to use minority languages in private institutions, including schools and universities. But it does not require the state to provide publicly funded minority language education, which is precisely what many linguistic minorities claim is necessary for their linguistic survival.

Education is an especially contentious feature of linguistic diversity dilemmas because both the state and the minority tend to view it as central to the realization of their collective aspirations. In so far as language provides the medium through which social norms are articulated and communicated it is the glue which binds together individual members of a community. Following on from this, it is often assumed that without a common language a community will begin to lose its cohesiveness. A way to avoid this unhappy scenario is to ensure that children are proficient in the language of the community to which they belong, which is precisely why education has long been a focal point of both civic and ethnic nation-building. But in situations of linguistic diversity, which language community should children properly belong to, the language of the home or the language of the state, and who shall decide?

This dilemma was already apparent in the League of Nations System of Minority Guarantees which required publicly funded primary education in minority languages where numbers warranted. Should the state determine which children belonged to a minority and thus have a right to attend minority language schools? Or is this a matter for parents to decide? In 1928 the Permanent Court of International Justice attempted to resolve such disputes by ruling in the Upper Silesia Schools Case that whether or not a person belonged to a minority was a 'question of fact not of will', the implication being that ultimately states (and not parents) determined who was and who was not a minority. Inherent within such controversies is the continuing fear that individuals cannot fully belong to more than one language community such that bilingualism may be viewed as a threat by minority and majority alike.

For all of these reasons, the key standard-setting documents in the area of minority rights are much more muted when it comes to state-funded minority language education. Article 27 of the ICCPR includes no reference to education. Article 4(3) of the UN Declaration on Minorities acknowledges that it would be desirable for states to 'take appropriate measures so that, wherever possible, persons belonging to minorities may have adequate opportunities to learn their mother tongue or to have instruction in their mother tongue' but does not require such action.

The main European standard-setting documents in the area of minority rights are somewhat more forthcoming with respect to state-funded minority language education. So, for example, article 15 of the Framework Convention for the Protection of National Minorities recognizes that 'every person belonging to a . . . minority has the right to learn his or her minority language'. In areas inhabited by minorities either traditionally or in substantial numbers, and where there is sufficient demand, states 'shall endeavour to ensure . . . adequate opportunities for being taught in the minority language or for receiving instruction in this language'. However, such requirements apply only within the framework of existing educational systems and 'without prejudice to the learning of the official language or teaching in this language'. Similarly, article 8 of the European Charter for Regional or Minority Languages identifies a range of educational policies which states might use to support minority languages. Here too, however, states are given a significant latitude in implementing these recommendations. They are free to select not only the particular policies best suited for their own domestic circumstances but also what minority languages within their territory shall be included under the Charter's rubric.

The right to be understood by the state

The most controversial component of minority language claims is the right to be understood by the state, its institutions, agencies and officials. It is at this point that the demand for minority language rights in effect becomes a demand for equal recognition alongside the existing authoritative language of state. The ultimate outcome of such proposals would thus be a version of official linguistic pluralism (i.e., bilingualism or multilingualism) where more than one language would be accorded authoritative status by the state. There are numerous domestic examples of such linguistic arrangements, as has already been discussed under the section 'Multicultural language' on pp. 115–16. But in all of these cases, the state has by its own sovereign will decided to adopt an official policy of linguistic pluralism. The idea that states should be obliged to enter into such arrangements when it is contrary to their perceived national interest (i.e., when the majority and its representative government is opposed to these measures) is altogether more problematic.

Thus, here too, international minority rights standard-setting documents are much more muted in their recommendations than with respect to the more basic right to speak a minority language. Article 14 of the ICCPR provides minimal translation rights to those individuals charged with a criminal offence. Such accused have the right to 'be informed promptly and in detail in a language which he understands of the nature and cause of the charge against him' and are entitled 'to have the free assistance of an interpreter if he cannot understand or speak the language used in court'. Similar requirements can be found in article 6 of the ECHR and in article 10(3) of the Framework Convention.

At the other extreme, general rights to effective participation may be found in a number of minority rights texts. Article 2(3) of the UN Declaration on Minorities stipulates: 'Persons belonging to minorities have the right to participate effectively in decisions on the national and, where appropriate, regional level concerning the minority to which they belong or the regions in which they live, in a manner not incompatible with national legislation.' Similarly, article 15 of the Framework Convention calls on states to 'create the conditions necessary for the effective participation of persons belonging to national minorities in cultural, social and economic life and in public affairs, in particular those affecting them'. These clauses have been interpreted as evidence of the growing normative recognition that some opportunities for minority language participation within or access to state institutions is a necessary component of minority protection.

Specific stipulations to this effect, however, are less common within the various standard-setting documents and, even where they do exist, are usually formulated in a more conditional wording such that states retain a significant latitude of discretion in these areas. For example, article 10(2) of the Framework Convention provides that 'in areas inhabited by . . . minorities traditionally or in substantial numbers' and only 'if those persons so request' and 'where such a request corresponds to a real need', states 'shall endeavour to ensure, *as far as possible* [emphasis added], the conditions which would make it possible to use the minority language in relations between those persons and the administrative authorities'. Similarly, while the European Charter for Regional or Minority Languages contains an extensive list of suggested minority language practices in the area of judicial authorities (article 9) and administrative authorities and public services (article 10), state signatories are only obliged to implement one of these provisions. That is considerably less than the three provisions which must be implemented with respect to education (article 8) and cultural facilities (article 12).

Conclusion

Language policy in general, including any particular response to the existence of linguistic minorities, reflects the prevailing construction of political community. Where political community is constructed from above, linguistic diversity is relatively unproblematic and may therefore be ignored, tolerated or even supported as ruling interests dictate. Where political community is constructed from below and authority is located in the people, linguistic diversity has historically been more problematic. This more contentious relationship is apparent in the related discourses of civic and ethnic language, both of which, albeit for somewhat different reasons, privilege the ideal of a single linguistic community as an essential component of popular sovereignty.

The minority rights response to linguistic diversity dilemmas aims to balance the requirements of the authoritative language of state against the desire of minority language speakers to preserve their own distinct linguistic community. At its most basic, this involves the recognition of a right to speak a minority language in addition to the more general right to freedom of expression. Such minority language arrangements are intended to coexist alongside the authoritative language of state and it is understood that states should retain the right to preserve and promote the authoritative language as the necessary medium for public communication. Requirements for state-funded minority language education and for a right to be understood by the state are far more controversial because they begin to intrude on the linguistic monopoly of the authoritative language within public life.

5
Ethnicity

Introduction

Ethnicity may be defined as 'origin by birth or descent' (*OED* 1989). It pertains to 'common racial, cultural, religious or linguistic characteristics' (*OED* 1989) and may be used to 'designate a group within a larger system' (*OED* 1989). The underlying logic of ethnicity presumes humankind is naturally divided into various kin-groups, each of which possesses its own particular physical and cultural traits which are passed on from one generation to the next thus ensuring some degree of continuity across historical time. This way of looking at the world owes much to the nineteenth century conviction that humanity was intrinsically and not merely superficially characterized by diversity and that heredity could provide insight into social as well as physical differences between peoples. Consequently, the word 'ethnic' did not acquire its current meaning until the middle of the nineteenth century; prior to that time, its usage was quite different and signified groups that were non-Christian, i.e. heathen or pagan (*OED* 1989).

Accordingly, the concept of ethnicity is a relatively recent invention and should not be confused with the ethnic characteristics associated with it. Ethnic characteristics themselves (including religion, language and shared physical traits) are a common feature of community and evidence of them can be found throughout human history. But it is important to remember that such characteristics are nevertheless distinct from the concept of ethnicity even though they may help to define it. Ethnicity is a contemporary social category like class and thus prescriptive as well as descriptive (Glazer and Moynihan 1975: 2–3). It contains underlying postulates about the way humanity ought to be organized which privileges some relationships over others. This in turn reminds us that there is nothing intrinsically politically salient about ethnic characteristics as such. Instead, these characteristics only become politicized in the context of particular normative assumptions about the way political, social and economic life ought to be organized.

Ethnicity as a diversity dilemma

Prior to the emergence of popular sovereignty towards the end of the eighteenth century, ethnic identities and attachments were for the most part relatively unimportant as political issues. This is not to suggest that such identities didn't matter but rather that they didn't matter in the same way or to the same degree that they do now. Individual men and women possessed what we today describe as ethnic characteristics and presumably valued the identifications and associations that went with them. However, political authority as such was not predicated upon a shared ethnicity and so ethnic diversity was comparatively far less problematic. Those in power did not claim to rule on the basis of an affinity with their subject population but rather on a mandate from a higher authority of some kind, be this human or divine.

Once authority was located in the people, however, it became imperative to establish a common bond between the members of a community and their political rulers, and to separate one community from another. Ethnic characteristics afforded a readily available means of doing precisely that and were therefore used as building blocks for the construction of yet another new social category – the nation – in whom popular sovereignty was presumed to reside. Thus a nation came to be defined as 'an extensive aggregate of persons, so closely associated with each other by common descent, language, or history, as to form a distinct race or people, usually organized as a separate political state and occupying a definite territory' (*OED* 1989). As we shall see, the public prominence and significance of ethnic characteristics varies in important respects between the different varieties of nation which have been imagined. Nevertheless, in each of these circumstances, ethnic traits such as language have been used to create and sustain political communities.

The current political controversy attached to ethnies and ethnicity is derived from their affinity with nations and nationalism. Since the nation-state in all its forms places a premium upon social conformity with those characteristics which define its collective identity and thus support its claim to popular sovereignty, the existence of ethnic minorities in this context is almost unavoidably problematic, by which I mean it necessitates a political response of some kind. At the same time, and also as a consequence of the new norm of popular sovereignty and its concomitant ideology of nationalism, ethnic minorities in many different countries and circumstances have asserted their ethnic distinctiveness and on this basis claimed political rights, including equality, identity and even self-determination. In other words, both states and minorities have engaged with the new politics of nationalism and so ethnicity has itself become politicized.

As a result, ethnic diversity within states has come to be viewed as a potential challenge to the territorial and political status quo on which the prevailing political order is based. Accordingly, states have responded with various minority policies designed to prevent instability and fragmentation. While the common purpose of all such programmes is the preservation of the current political status quo, the means to this end vary enormously as between the recognition and the elimination of diversity.

Ethnic belonging within community

Broadly speaking, political community can be constructed in one of two ways – as a community of putative descent, or as a community of putative consent. In a community of putative descent, the social bond between members is imagined as a bond of kinship or blood. Whether or not the members of such a community are in scientific fact genetically or biologically similar is not at issue; rather what matters is that they subscribe to a myth of common descent and that this myth supports and sustains the social obligations between them. In a community of putative consent, the social bond between members is imagined as a bond of law or promise. Whether or not the members of such a community are in historic fact linked by an actual contract or other act of consent is not at issue; rather what matters is that they subscribe to a myth of consent and that this myth supports and sustains the social obligations between them.

Ethnic characteristics are likely to arise in both normative circumstances as a consequence of sustained social interaction through time. People who live together long enough will almost unavoidably develop a common pattern of life peculiar to themselves. In such circumstances, anthropologists and sociologists would expect to find evidence of shared myths and memories, local customs, rituals, dialects, manner of dress, cuisine and so forth. But the political significance attached to these common practices is quite different as between communities of putative descent and communities of putative consent. In a community of putative descent, ethnic characteristics are likely to be viewed as tangible evidence of the imagined cosanguinity. Those who do not possess these characteristics do not share in the common descent and thus cannot be members of the community – differences in dress, dialect and so forth thus denote an almost impenetrable barrier between members and the outside world. It is usually very difficult for those outside the kin-group to join a community of putative descent without in some ceremonial way entering into the blood relationship which underscores it (for instance, by marriage or blood oath). In contrast, while dress, dialect and so forth may still distinguish members from non-members within a community of putative consent, membership is in principle at least open to anyone who is prepared to bind themselves to the prevailing social contract. Thus, in a community of putative descent, ethnic identity is intrinsic to belonging, whereas in a community of putative consent, ethnic identity is merely derivative of belonging. Accordingly, the existence of ethnic diversity is likely to be comparatively more controversial in a community of putative descent than it is in a community of putative consent.

Ethnic belonging and medieval universitas

Within the medieval universitae, community was constructed in terms of religion and so religious faith was the main arbiter of difference. In this sense, then, such a universitas privileges one particular ethnic characteristic over all others and makes this the decisive element of belonging. There are of course examples of religious communities based on putative descent – usually from the original or founding members of the religion (for instance, the Jews or the Druze). But significantly, none of the great medieval universitae operated in this way. Instead, these were communities of putative consent and thus membership was open to all who were prepared to bind themselves through an act of faith.

Thus, for example, in the Christian Gospel of St Matthew Jesus instructs his disciples to 'Go ye therefore, and teach all nations, baptizing them in the name of the Father, and of the Son, and of the Holy Ghost' (Matthew: 28: 19). The word translated as 'nations' in the King James Version of the Bible is the Greek *ethne*. The expression used for 'all nations' in the original Greek translation is *panta ta ethne*, which literally means all the peoples of the world. Whether translated as gentiles, nations or peoples, it is apparent that salvation through the Christian religion is open to all (Showalter 1996: 2). It is precisely on this basis that Bartolomé de las Casas defended the indigenous peoples of the Americas as human beings of the same intrinsic worth as their Spanish conquerors: both were capable of receiving the divine truth (de las Casas 2003).

Similarly, anyone can become a Muslim by making a public declaration of belief in Islam. Indeed, the word 'Muslim' simply means 'one who submits' and thus has no particular ethnic connotation (Maqsood 2003: 1). Accordingly, there are numerous historic examples of ethnically European Christian converts to Islam attaining positions of importance within Islamic communities – for instance, the Count de Bonneval converted to Islam in 1729 taking the name Ahmed, entered the Ottoman service and within ten years attained the rank of *pasha* (Lewis 1982: 49–50).

The fact that both medieval Christianity and Islam constructed belonging in this way – that is through a myth of putative consent – owes much to the previous classical traditions of ancient Greece and Rome. Here it is perhaps important to recall that Christianity and Islam share a dual normative inheritance – each is at one and the same time an heir both to the Judaic and the classical traditions. Christian and Islamic universalism have their origins in the prophetic monotheism of Hebraic thought (Bozeman 1960: 232).

> The notion that God ruled the world by delegating important functions to a special people by virtue of a special covenant came to the Christians and Moslims [sic] who adopted the wisdom of the Holy Book. And each of these three religious groups [Jews, Christians and Muslims] was convinced, thenceforth, that it, and it alone, had been set apart deliberately and from all other groups of human beings and constituted, therefore, the center of the universe. (Bozeman 1960: 233)

But unlike Judaism, whose covenant was limited to a particular chosen people united in a common descent from the original tribes of Israel, the revealed truth of Christianity and Islam was believed to be for all humankind without distinction. In other words, both Christianity and Islam were 'travelling religions' whose appeal transcended local ties of kinship.

As a result, Christians and Muslims turned to the classical belief in law and contract as the basis for social relations within their respective medieval universitae (Bozeman 1960: 210–12). The myth that sustained Rome was a conviction that otherwise diverse ethnic groups had been united first by Aeneas and later by Romulus through a common law; accordingly, membership was in theory open to all who accepted Roman law and agreed to be bound by it (Geary 2002: 49–50). Following on from this, in the Roman tradition distinct concepts were employed to distinguish communities united by choice from those united by birth – Romans were a *populus* while the inhabitants of Europe beyond the Rhine were variously described as *gens*, *natio*, or *tribus* (Geary 2002: 50–1). This corresponds with the older Greek distinction between *politicos* or those who govern themselves by law and *ethnos* or those who govern themselves according to custom (such as by descent) (Hannaford 1996: 22–8). To be *ethne* was to be outside Greek civilization and its tradition of *nomos* (law).

Christians and Muslims took this classical approach to community through consent and imbued it with their own religious convictions – the law became a divine and not merely a civic creation. To submit to the law of the Catholic Church or the law of Islam was to submit to God's will and not merely the will of mortal men in their guise as citizens. Accordingly, in the early Christian Church, it was those groups who lived without the divine truth as revealed by Jesus Christ who were deemed *ethne* (Ghebali 1998). To be *ethne* was in this context to be outside Christian civilization and its tradition of natural law. Indeed, Latin Christendom was built piecemeal over many centuries after the fall of Rome by the missionary conversion of European pagans or *ethne*, typically kings and other rulers, to Christianity; in becoming Christians, kings subjected themselves and the populations they ruled to the Christian god and his law, representatives and agents on earth (Jackson 2000: 158).

The classical legal order of the Mediterranean world which had previously been based on Roman law was thus superseded by the Christian natural law and the Islamic shariah. The consequence of this transformation was to render ethnic diversity relatively unproblematic provided religious dogma was maintained; conversely, however, once religious dogma acquired the force of law, the existence of religious minorities took on an entirely new significance. As communities of putative consent (in the form of a personal submission to divine authority), neither Christianity nor Islam views the diverse ethnic origins of its members as a potential threat to belonging. All Christians, regardless of ethnicity, are brothers and sisters in Christ. Similarly, all Muslims, regardless of ethnicity, are members of the Islamic *ummah* or family of the faithful. Instead, as has already been discussed in the chapter on religion, the diversity dilemmas which are likely to arise in the context of political authority constructed on a religious basis will be disproportionately concerned with religious minorities – for example, Jews and Muslims in Christendom or Christians and Jews in Islam – and not with ethnic minorities.

Ethnic belonging and dynasty

The dynastic idea of belonging was also primarily one of consent and not one of descent. The dynastic state which emerged out of the prior Christian universitas adopted many of the trappings of the old order that it sought to replace – including a belief in law as the foundation of community. In medieval Europe the ultimate source of authority was the Christian god, whose natural law was universal and so extended over all humanity irrespective of ethnicity. Equally so, in theory at least, was the rule of his two representatives on earth – the pope and the Holy Roman Emperor. From them the system of delegated feudal authority spread downwards but each vassal always held his office by virtue of prerogative conferred from above (Macartney 1934: 35).

What has been called the feudal order of medieval Europe was based upon putative consent rather than cosanguinity. In other words, this was a community of promise rather than one of blood or kinship: it was formally predicated upon a 'personal bond based on an oath of allegiance' (Schulze 1998: 7). In practice, of course, an individual's position in the hierarchy of feudal society was largely determined by birth. Nowhere is this more evident than in the institution of serfdom, where a single act of submission could bind not only the individual concerned but all his descendants (Southern 1993: 96–7). Similarly, the solidarity of kinship remained strong. For example, the place of the 'blood feud' in penal law (whereby the family of a murdered person could exact revenge on the family of the murderer) persisted (albeit with increasing restrictions) into the twelfth century, until it was finally extinguished by royal prerogative (Bloch 1961: 142).

Nevertheless, social relationships based exclusively on blood were foreign to and inconsistent with the normative characteristic of feudalism (Bloch 1961: 123). The myth which underpinned social relations at every level was one of consent.

> Medieval society was prolific in creating forms of association to which entry was obtained by oath . . . The serf's unhappy freedom from law was involuntary [provided this status was inherited and not directly entered into by the individual concerned] but the submission of the knight, the baron, the clerk, the monk, the burgess, to their various codes of law was voluntary. The nobleman was bound by several codes of law – as a Christian, a baron, a knight, a subject of the king; and he could suffer all manner of penalties for a breach of any of these codes of law. Into all of these obligations he had entered by an

individual contract in the ceremonies of baptism, homage, knighthood and fealty. If he was punished, even by being burnt as a heretic, he could reflect that he was being punished for a breach of contract. (Southern 1993: 107)

Any ethnic similarity or difference between members of feudal society was irrelevant to the social bonds between them, which remained grounded in law. At issue in such feudal relationships was personal submission and obedience, not imagined cosanguinity. It is this view of social relations which the dynastic princes inherited from the feudal age and ultimately adapted to their own purpose, namely the creation of territorially cohesive kingdoms under a single, central government which recognized no superior.

It is important to recall that in this period theology and politics were closely united in both theory and practice such that the prevailing idea of kingship was a part of Christian doctrine (Figgis 1922: 11–12). In medieval Europe, kings were viewed as 'God's anointed' specially chosen by the Christian god to rule over men. This view of kingship is apparent in the coronation ceremonies through which a new king was crowned:

He was anointed with the holy oil used in the consecration of priests; he was invested with the ring and staff conferred on bishops, with the power to destroy heresies and to unite his subjects in the Catholic faith [or after the Protestant Reformation in whatever Christian faith the prince chose]; and he received the sword and sceptre with words which gave the highest authority to his use of violence. (Southern 1993: 91)

As dynastic princes began to challenge the pope's assertion of supreme authority within Christendom and to claim for themselves supremacy within their kingdoms, many of the earlier ceremonial acts associated with coronation (which might suggest the continued pre-eminence of the pope as head of the Catholic Church) were rejected or fell into abeyance. But the belief that a king ruled by divine right persisted and was, if anything, made even more prominent by the new dynastic rulers. 'The right to the Crown was no longer that of election or coronation, but that of the next heir whom God alone can make . . . the Crown had become a birthright'

(Figgis 1922: 27). As James I of England reminded his Parliament in 1610: 'The state of monarchy is the supremest thing upon earth; for kings are not only God's lieutenants upon earth and sit upon God's throne, but even by God himself they are called gods' (Oakley 1988: 105).

Out of what was in its origins an essentially theological view of kingship emerged a new understanding of political authority better suited to the centralizing aims of the dynastic princes: the theory of sovereignty. Sovereignty is 'the idea that there is a final and absolute authority in the political community . . . and no final and absolute authority exists elsewhere' (Hinsley 1966: 26). In the dynastic period, sovereignty was understood to be 'vested in a single person [the prince] by God and . . . resistance to the sovereign [was] the worst of sins' (Figgis 1922: 45). The idea of sovereignty gave legal authority and moral purpose to the state-building endeavours of the dynastic princes: *rex est imperator in regno suo* – 'the king is emperor in his own realm' – became the motto of the age.

At the beginning and throughout their history, the great dynastic families of Europe – Tudor, Valois, Bourbon, Habsburg, Wittlesbach, Hohenzollern, Savoy, Romanov, and so forth – were motivated by territory, wealth, prestige and power (Shafer 1955: 62–3). Their political purpose was to consolidate and wherever possible extend their dynastic possessions. This objective they accomplished through war, conquest, purchase, inheritance, marriage, diplomacy, duplicity, and the legal and illegal confiscation of feudal vassals' property. Yet at no point was the legitimacy of dynastic rule over territories acquired in this way challenged on the basis of ethnicity. The theory of sovereignty was 'formulated to fit actual circumstances, which were those of kings who were ruling over territories which were not racially homogeneous. Hobbes's Leviathan contains no single word hinting at any impropriety in an English king ruling over Welsh or Irish subjects . . .' (Macartney 1934: 38–9). That is because authority was vested in the person of the prince, who ruled by inherited and ultimately divinely sanctioned right. From this perspective, the ethnic identity of the subject population was largely irrelevant and inconsequential – obedience was owed to the king regardless of any ethnic bond between ruler and ruled. The principle of *cujus regio, ejus religio* – like sovereign, like religion – which after 1648 became a foundational principle of relations between sovereigns embodies precisely this assumption.

Dynastic princes were not intent upon building what we would today term nations – indeed the modern social category of the nation and the theory of political authority which underscores it (popular sovereignty) had yet to be imagined. The main objective of sovereigns like Henry VIII or Louis XIV was to enlarge their territory and increase their political control over it. It was *étatisme* not nationalism which characterized the ambitions of the Tudors and the Valois and the other dynasties (Shafer 1955: 68).

> They were intent on overcoming authority which impeded and rivaled their own, and their efforts were directed quite as much against the great feudal lords of their own nationality as against the chieftains of the minorities. If for example the Estates of Brittany had to complain of repeated violations of their original pact with the King of France, the Estates of other, purely French, provinces suffered no less heavily. (Macartney 1934: 39–40)

Where dynastic state building consolidated those traits which would subsequently become constitutive of a common national identity (as for example when Henry VIII and Louis XIV recognized a single dynastic language as authoritative throughout their respective kingdoms to the exclusion of all others), it did so for dynastic rather than ethnic calculations. Such policies were intended to enforce the central dynastic authority over what had hitherto been separate feudal fiefdoms (like Wales and Brittany) and not in the first instance to nationalize the populations within them. That process of assimilation which we would today call nationalization was in England and Wales under Henry VIII and in France under Louis XIV an unintended consequence of dynastic centralization. The dynastic princes harboured no particular ill will against their ethnic minorities, expecting from them no more than the usual obedience required of all their subjects (Macartney 1932: 41). Instead, as one might expect given the continued emphasis on religion as the ultimate source of political authority, those diversity dilemmas which arose during the dynastic period were disproportionately concerned with religious minorities – Jews and Muslims in Spain, Huguenots in France, Catholics in England and so on.

Thus while the dynastic idea includes an emphasis on cosanguinity in the form of the dynastic family with territorial possessions being transferred across generations within that family on the basis of inheritance, the bond between sovereign and subject is nevertheless imagined as one of law and not ethnicity. Anyone of whatever ethnicity who found themselves within the territory of the dynastic prince was subject to his rule and owed obedience to his commands. In this context, territories and populations were assumed to be one and the same. What mattered was the historical relationship between territory and crown; whether or not the peoples who inhabited such territories shared an ethnic bond with the prince who ruled them was entirely irrelevant. The constitutional distinction drawn in 1830 between a king of France and a king of the French would have been meaningless in the dynastic period (Reynolds 1990: 259). Indeed, the dynastic states forming out of medieval Christendom in the fifteenth and sixteenth centuries came to be known, in the first instance, by the title of their chief province and not by the ethnicity of the peoples who occupied their territories; France was named for the Île de France, Poland for Polonia, etc. It was the experience of sharing a single law and government which promoted a sense of solidarity amongst the subjects within a given dynastic kingdom and not their real or imagined ethnic similarity (Reynolds 1990: 253).

Ethnic belonging and nation

The nation in its current usage is a social category invented to answer that most vexing of modern political conundrums: 'who are the people in whom sovereignty resides?' It is important to remember that no one even thought to ask this question until the idea of dynastic sovereignty was challenged by a new principle of political authority, namely popular sovereignty. While the divine right of kings prevailed, an ethnically German prince ruling over a motley assortment of German, Slavic and Hungarian peoples seemed a perfectly reasonable arrangement. After the rise of popular sovereignty, however, political communities like the Habsburg Empire appeared not only anachronistic but downright abhorrent. As with the dynastic ideal which it challenged and ultimately displaced, popular sovereignty was both a response to and a catalyst for changing political circumstances. But once accepted as the dominant paradigm of political authority, it rendered the continued existence of dynastic rule increasingly untenable. In so doing, it politicized popular identity and by extension also ethnicity in ways hitherto unimaginable.

The principle of popular sovereignty began to emerge in England in the late seventeenth century but was not fully formulated until the second half of the eighteenth century. At about this time, the medieval theory of authority and its concomitant political identities of sovereign and subject were increasingly questioned by political theorists and reformers. Initially, this challenge came from English Parliamentarians and political philosophers in the context of the Civil War of the 1640s. Thus, for example, Thomas Hobbes refuted the divine origins of dynastic sovereignty and instead put forward the idea that the only essential quality of the sovereign was the capacity to compel obedience. This new way of conceptualizing political authority led, later on, to the conclusion that such power could not safely be entrusted to just one man, or even to a few men, because the temptation to abuse it would be too great. Instead, it was argued that sovereignty should properly be vested in parliament which was 'neither one nor few' (Bailyn 1992: 200).

It was this view of political authority which triumphed in England in what has become known as the Glorious Revolution of 1688–9. At that time, the English Parliament deposed the reigning Stuart monarch (James II) and replaced him with the Dutch Prince William of Orange and his wife Mary Stuart (daughter of James I), who jointly acceded to the English throne as William III and Mary II. The only justification which could convincingly be made for such a radical act was that ultimate sovereignty resided in the people not the prince and thus parliament as representative of the people could transfer it from one prince to another when circumstances required (Trevelyan 1965). A century later, the American and French revolutionaries explained themselves in precisely these terms. As James Madison wrote in 1792, 'In Europe, charters of liberty have been granted by power. America has set the example and France has followed it, of charters of power granted by liberty' (Bailyn 1992: 55).

It is at this point in the history of political ideas that the concept of the nation achieves political salience. Who are the people in whom sovereignty, and indeed liberty, ultimately resides? The people are the nation and the state exists as an expression of the national will. 'The principle of all sovereignty rests essentially in the nation. No body and no individual may exercise authority which does not emanate from the nation expressly' (article 3, 1789 Declaration of the Rights of Man and of the Citizen). Moreover, 'for a nation thus abused to arise unanimously and to resist their prince, even to the dethroning of him, is not criminal but a reasonable way of vindicating their liberties and just rights' (Jonathan Mayhew, 1750 as quoted in Bailyn 1992: 93).

The nation as a contested concept   These are grand words and their political resonance echoes down the centuries to the present time. Yet while the belief that the 'people are the nation and the state exists as an expression of the national will' has inspired many hitherto subject peoples, it offers little guidance in determining which collectivities may reasonably claim a right to sovereignty and which may not. In other words 'this is an imperfect solution of the ancient problem: where does sovereignty lie?' (Hinsley 1966: 157). That is because 'the nation' remains a fundamentally contested concept which can be defined either as a community of putative consent or as a community of putative descent. Nations of putative consent, which Hans Kohn has described as 'civic nations', are imagined as 'unions of citizens, by the will of the individuals who expressed it in contracts, covenants or plebiscites' (Kohn 1960: 351). In contrast, nations of putative descent, which Kohn terms 'ethnic nations', are imagined as 'folk communities, formed by the ties of a hoary past, and later of prehistoric, biological factors' (Kohn 1960: 351).

This difference is epitomized in the distinction between *jus solis* (right of soil) and *jus sanguinis* (right of blood) in determining citizenship (Brubaker 1992). Although these are ideal types, they nevertheless remain useful in explaining the normative distinctions between a nation imagined as a community of putative consent and a nation imagined as a community of putative descent (Grieco 2002).

In a *jus solis* system, citizenship is based on place of birth.

Although there are exceptions to this rule, in general, people born within the territory of the state (hence on its 'soil') are citizens, while people born outside the boundaries of the state (on 'foreign soil') are non-citizens. Thus, in a *jus solis* context, the term 'foreign born' refers to residents of a state who were born in another country. Foreign-born residents can, under certain circumstances, change their status and become citizens through consent in a process of naturalization. When combined, both place of birth and citizenship status can be used to divide the population of civic nation-states into three categories – native-born citizens, foreign-born citizens and non-citizens – and define who among the foreign born has acquired the full rights and responsibilities of political membership. Thus, for example, according to US Code 1401–1409 (1986), any child born within the territory of the United States, regardless of the citizenship of the parents, is a US citizen. In addition, US citizenship may be acquired by those born elsewhere on the fulfilment of certain conditions, including lawful residence in the United States for at least five years; the ability to speak, read and write English; evidence of good moral character; and familiarity with US history and culture.

In a *jus sanguinis* system, descent plays a pivotal role in defining who is and who can become a citizen. Where people were born is not important. Whether or not they can trace their ancestry (through ties of 'blood') back to the ethnic nation is important. In this context, the term 'foreigner' refers to those in the population who do not share in the 'blood' of the nation. In general, under *jus sanguinis* citizenship policies, it is usually difficult for those without blood connections to become naturalized citizens even if they were born on the territory of the state or are long-term residents within it. In contrast, it is generally far easier for co-ethnics born in other states to obtain citizenship upon returning to their ancestral homeland, in some cases even if their families have lived elsewhere for generations. Thus, for example, the German Citizenship Law of 1913, which until very recently formed the basis of citizenship in the German Federal Republic, states that citizenship will be inherited (Klusmeyer 1993). This law was intended to make it impossible for the significant Jewish and Polish minorities who resided in the Kaiserreich at that time to acquire German citizenship (Wertheimer 1987). Whereas in civic nations it is possible for ethnic minorities to be incorporated into the body politic provided that they demonstrate an ability and willingness to abide by the law and to participate in the prevailing political culture, in ethnic nations those minorities who do not share in the imagined cosanguinity will, by definition, never fully belong.

Civic nation-states When the popularly sovereign nation was first invented in Britain, France and the United States, it was imagined territorially in keeping with earlier dynastic practices. Accordingly, the myth underscoring these political communities is one of consent and not descent – so, for example, America's 'founding fathers' (George Washington, Thomas Jefferson, James Madison and so forth) are not remembered for their role as physical primogenitors but as constitution makers. Indeed, in contemporary English usage nationality is a synonym for citizenship as distinct from ethnic or racial origin in keeping with the principle of *jus solis*. National identity in the civic tradition is primarily defined through a shared political experience and common constitutional guarantees. Linguistic or cultural programmes are generally understood in terms of civic virtues and not the defence of ethnic purity per se.

The civic nation-state tends to relegate ethnicity to the private sphere. Minority ethnic identities may be tolerated within the home, where distinct languages, traditions, myths and memories may be preserved provided these do not conflict with or in any way undermine the prevailing civic culture. Obviously, such private identities do not receive public recognition from the civic nation-state. Instead, public institutions actively support the civic national culture and language within public life to the exclusion of all others. And where necessary in defence of this civic culture, assimilationist or paternal policies may be directed towards non-conformist ethnic groups.

Assimilation into the dominant Anglo-Saxon culture was the common experience of immigrant minorities in Canada, Australia and the United States during the early part of the twentieth century. This process is nowhere more apparent than in the changing public identities of the immigrants themselves. My two grandfathers are representative of what was a much larger social trend – in each case not only their surnames but also their given names were anglicized to fit prevailing social mores. Johannes Pedar Jokumsen (born in Denmark in 1895 and emigrated to the United States in 1912) became John Peter Jackson and Josip Stanislav Prpic (born in Croatia in 1903 and emigrated to Canada in 1921) became Joseph Stanley Perpick. The anglicization of 'foreign' names was part of a social process that transformed immigrants of many diverse ethnic backgrounds into Canadians, Australians and Americans with rights to full participation in the body politic.

At about this same time, ethnic minorities deemed insufficiently 'civilized' for citizenship in the short or medium term often found themselves objects of paternalist policies intended to help them 'mature' into full members of the body politic. Such minorities were subject to separate administrative arrangements distinct from the regular governmental structure of the civic nation-state and with limited consent or participation from the minorities themselves. These practices were commonplace in European overseas empires. Similar arrangements once existed for the indigenous populations of Canada and the United States, who were in each case effectively wards of the federal government. The ultimate objective of such endeavours was purportedly to produce free and equal citizens, even though these were often assumed to be several generations removed from the men, women and children initially subject to them. In other words, such paternalism was not generally conceived as a form of permanent exclusion from the body politic but as a precursor to eventual incorporation within it.

Ethnic nation-states The same cannot be said of minority policies within ethnic nation-states. In such situations, political membership is determined by purportedly 'natural' and thus innate characteristics which by definition cannot be changed by assimilation or tutelage. The individual no longer determines his or her nation: instead, the nation determines the individual. Thus, although the freedom of minorities to express and develop their distinct ethnic identities may be limited in either civic or ethnic nation-states, the latter are arguably far more hostile towards ethnic minorities and thus potentially more destructive not only of ethnic minority identities but in extreme circumstances even of their physical survival.

Such an illiberal outcome to the new politics of popular sovereignty and its nationalist ideology was not immediately anticipated. Instead, it was initially assumed that this principle would everywhere create self-ruling civic nations following the earlier British, French and American models. Again, John Stuart Mill is instructive:

> Where the sentiment of nationality exists in any force, there is a *prime facie* case for uniting all the members of the nationality under the same government, a government to themselves apart. This is merely saying that the question of government ought to be decided by the governed. One hardly knows what any division of the human race should be free to do, if not to determine with which of the various collective bodies of human beings they choose to associate themselves. (Mill 1999: 392)

Mill, and nineteenth century liberals like him, viewed freedom and national identity as natural allies in the fight against dynastic empires and other forms of non-representative government.

The various national movements in Central, Southern and Eastern Europe demanded the union of ethnic nations divided by dynastic empire and the separation of other ethnic nations suppressed within dynastic empire. This ethnic interpretation was the logical translation of the civic democratic idea to the political realities pertaining outside Western Europe and its North American colonies. Where dynamic state-building monarchies had not arisen in the medieval period, there was generally no ready-made civic basis in which popular sovereignty could take root and flourish. Polyglot empires that continued to base their rule on ancient dynastic rights arising from marriage, succession, purchase, conquest etc. with little regard for either constitutions or representative institutions confronted many of the new revolutionaries. How then could the 'will of the people' be expressed and developed in circumstances like those prevailing in much of the Habsburg Empire where territories were far-flung and scattered, central administration was weak and civic institutions were largely absent? The answer was of course to develop an alternative basis on which to mobilize popular support and action: a myth of putative common descent.

Western liberals expected the new nation-states achieved in this way to practise representative government and guarantee the rights of the individual: the new revolutionaries tended to have somewhat different ideas about the priority of individual freedoms (Namier 1963: 38–9). For example, Giuseppe Mazzini, intellectual leader of the Italian Risorgimento, saw the collective interest of the nation as more fundamental than the rights of the individual:

> The epoch of individuality is concluded [wrote Mazzini in 1832]. It has been replaced by the epoch of the peoples. Individuality was a doctrine useful perhaps . . . in securing the exercise of some personal rights, but impotent to found nationality or association; and it is the duty of reformers to initiate the epoch of association. . . . The question of nationalities [meaning ethnic nations] is destined to give its name to the century. (Namier 1963: 39)

In other words, a new kind of political community was created in which the myth of putative descent was much more pronounced than hitherto. This new kind of community was not predicated upon a belief in individual autonomy as symbolized by a myth of consent but rather a commitment to the collective self as symbolized by descent, language and folk culture. Membership was therefore based on ties of blood (the *jus sanguinis*) rather than on the simple fact of being born within a particular sovereign jurisdiction (as per the *jus solis*).

Once the ethnic bond is accepted as the raison d'être of the state, ethnic diversity becomes a threat to popular sovereignty. When the right to rule is justified on the basis of an ethnic affinity between the population of a state and its government then the existence of ethnic minorities challenges the authority of those in power. In order to preserve its territorial integrity and domestic stability, the ethnic nation-state tends to act as if it is a homogeneous ethnic community. If (as is often the case) such a state is not in fact ethnically homogeneous, than it must 'endeavor to make the facts correspond to the ideal', regardless of the rights and liberties of those among its citizens who don't belong to the majority ethnic group (Cobban 1970: 109). At the same time, the reverse is also true: every ethnic nation or fraction thereof which is not an independent state must strive to become one. National survival is thus dependent upon the survival of the *ethnie* within its historic homeland.

Already in the 1848 movement for German unification one can discern the various dilemmas which arise in the context of building states on the basis of ethnic criteria. German unification was meaningless without a clear understanding as to which territories ought to be included in it. The answer adopted at the Frankfurt Assembly revealed an ethnic imperative: territories with predominantly German populations or German rulers would be included. This might at first glance seem a perfectly reasonable basis for admission – until, that is, one begins to ponder the anomalies. Switzerland had a significant German-speaking population and historic ties to the German-ruled Holy Roman Empire, but was nevertheless excluded from the list. Schleswig and Holstein had a significant Danish population and war over these provinces was only averted in 1848 by British and Russian intervention; such a war did eventually occur in 1864 and resulted in the loss of Danish territory to Prussia. Alsace could not be included without a war with France in 1870–1. Bohemia was a part of the German-ruled Habsburg Empire, but the majority of its population spoke Czech and a Czech nationalism as distinct from the German was already developing there (indeed, the Czech intellectuals led by the historian Palacký famously turned down an invitation to send a representative to the Frankfurt Assembly) (Seton-Watson 1977: 95). Ultimately, of course, the status of the German-speaking minority in the Sudetenland was used to justify the transfer of Czechoslovakian territory to Germany in 1938.

Such contradictions and controversies are by no means limited to the German example. Many territories claimed by Italian nationalists also had ethnic inconsistencies: Trieste and Trento, though majority Italian, nevertheless had significant minority populations (the former Slovene and the latter German); Istria and Dalmatia, though historically ruled by Venice, were populated almost exclusively by Croats and Serbs. Yet these territories became famous as the *Italia irredenta* (Italian unclaimed lands) – a slogan which later gave its name to the concept of irredentism (Seton-Watson 1977: 106–7).

At the same time, and also in response to the ethnic imperative, the circumstances of those ethnic minorities who eventually found themselves within the territories of the new ethnic nation-states became increasingly difficult. Indeed, the period between 1848 and 1945 – which we might term, following Mazzini, the 'century of nationalities' – was characterized by the widespread use of policies aimed at eliminating ethnic diversity within states. Where the myth of putative descent defines a political community, those groups who do not share its ascriptive characteristics cannot belong and therefore must be eliminated. This process of elimination can take different forms including ghettoization, expulsion or extermination. In each case, however, the end result is the same: the ethnic nation-state is 'cleansed' of its unwanted and potentially harmful ethnic minorities. Ghettoization is a practice which predates popular sovereignty – the origin of the term goes back to the medieval practice of confining Jews within particular quarters of otherwise Christian cities. It was notoriously revived by the Nazi regime as an element of their Final Solution against European Jewry. Expulsion featured prominently in Hitler's policy of *Lebensraum* and was also used by Stalin both within the Soviet Union itself as well as in Soviet-occupied Europe. Nor were such practices confined to authoritarian governments. At the Potsdam Conference in 1945 the 'Big Three' – Truman, Churchill and Stalin – unanimously endorsed the forced transfer of ethnic Germans from east of the Oder-Neisse line in order to preserve the post-war territorial status quo. Since the end of the Cold War, the practice has been most closely associated with events in former Yugoslavia from which the term 'ethnic cleansing' originates. The Jewish Holocaust remains the most widely known example of genocide, but there are both earlier (e.g., the Turkish genocide against the Armenians during World War I) and later (e.g., the Hutu genocide against the Tutsi in Rwanda during 1994) episodes.

The assumption underlying all of these responses is that political stability in an ethnic nation-state cannot tolerate ethnic diversity as such divisions will undermine the integrity of the overarching political order by calling into question the myth of common descent upon which it rests. In other words, this perspective views ethnicity in zero-sum terms such that coexistence between ethnic groups within the same jurisdiction is not an option. Although bleak, such an outlook nevertheless reflects a normative position: the well-being of individuals and their respective political communities is herein understood as dependent upon the fulfilment of ethnicity in the acquisition of separate, sovereign statehood, which in turn is seen to embody the 'natural order' in its purest form.

Ethnic belonging and empire

Ironically, the spread of nation-states and representative governments across Europe corresponded with the heyday of European overseas empire. So at the very moment when increasing numbers of Europeans were challenging the inherited rights of dynastic princes in the name of popular sovereignty, more and more peoples in Africa and Asia found themselves subject to colonial rule by Europeans. An empire is a political community in which 'supreme and extensive political dominion [is] exercised by a sovereign state over its dependencies' (*OED* 1989). This view of political authority has more in keeping with the feudal understanding of delegated power conferred from above than it does with the principle of popular sovereignty then current in the nineteenth century metropoles of London and Paris.

Like feudalism, imperialism was an arrangement grounded in law even though it was backed by disproportionate and sometimes brutal force. Thus, for example, Martin Wight is able to describe the constitutional structure of the British Empire in strict legal terms:

> The Dependent Empire is administered by the Colonial Office (and in one or two instances by the Commonwealth Relations Office) because it comes under the executive authority of the Crown. The legal forms and instruments by which it is administered are the same as those used in the general exercise of the Crown's executive powers. . . . The legal status of a dependency determines not only whether its constitution is derived from prerogative [executive decision] or statute, but also to some extent the legal instruments by which the constitution is established. (Wight 1952: 94)

Unlike the feudal order of medieval Europe, however, empire could not be grounded on consent precisely because those peoples subject to imperial rule were imagined as incapable of entering into social obligations of this kind. Instead, empire was based on an ideal of fiduciary obligation in which 'civilized peoples' assumed responsibility for those deemed 'inferior' on moral and material grounds. In other words, the 'promise' of colonial administration was unilateral on the part of the 'civilized' and not reciprocal – those peoples subject to it had little, if any, say in the matter. The myth which gave legitimacy to such paternal arrangements was the 'standard of civilization', according to which those states exercising governmental responsibilities over 'subject peoples' were responsible for protecting them against abuse, guaranteeing their political, economic, social and educational advancement, and guiding them towards eventual self-government. We see this standard embodied in article VI of the General Act of the Conference of Berlin (1885), in article 22 of the League of Nations Covenant (1919–24) with respect to the mandates system, and in article 73 of the UN Charter (1945) with respect to the trusteeship system.

How and in what manner these responsibilities should be carried out was a matter for the colonial authorities to determine subject only to external but not internal criticism. Colonial governments were not answerable to the population of those dependent territories over which they exercised imperial rule but rather to the central authority of the imperial metropole. The administration of the British Raj was therefore responsible to the Colonial Office in London, the Westminster Parliament and ultimately the British electorate – but not to the people of India themselves. Thus the moral approbation of public opinion within purportedly 'civilized' states was intended to perform that function of accountability which popular opinion within the colonial dependencies was denied – the fact that such approbation was either absent or ineffective as a check on the excesses of colonial rule points to a fundamental weakness in paternal arrangements of this kind.

The idea of empire per se is not predicated upon a shared ethnicity – far from it: empires are by definition political arrangements intended to incorporate diverse and often far-flung peoples under a single, central authority. Nevertheless, common beliefs – with respect to what made some peoples fit to rule themselves and others backward and thus incapable of self-government – were infused with ethnic assumptions. The nineteenth century 'standard of civilization' was a European invention and as such synonymous with European cultural values. While such values might be approximated by non-Europeans sufficiently 'educated' in western traditions, the growing influence of social Darwinist ideas about the significance of 'blood' and 'descent' made these categories increasingly difficult to fully transcend.

As a result, the day to day experience of European overseas empire for those colonial peoples subject to it often resembled a caste system: we see this reality vividly portrayed in J.S. Furnivall's classic study of colonialism in South-East Asia (Furnivall 1948). Imperialism facilitated and often encouraged the movement of peoples from one part of the empire to another. The result was a colonial jurisdiction with an indigenous majority, a ruling European minority and, in many cases, intermediate ethnic and racial minorities who had been introduced to provide economic services which the native population either would not or could not provide. So, for example, in the (British) Kenya colony Europeans controlled the colonial administration and key industries (such as the production and export of coffee); Asians ran the small and medium sized businesses; and Africans provided manual labour and domestic service. Although these different ethnic groups often lived in relatively close proximity to one another, their interaction was generally limited to the market place. According to Furnivall, plural societies like these lacked a unifying 'social will' and were only held together by a common economic system and by the threat or use of force (Nicholls 1974: 38–9).

In sum, European colonies in Africa and Asia were neither predicated upon consent nor in the first instance necessarily even single communities. While law may have regulated and legitimized imperial rule, an individual's social position within colonial society was largely determined by descent. And although ethnicity per se was not a justification of empire in and of itself, ethnic considerations nevertheless infused those ideas of moral and material progress that were used to justify European rule over non-European peoples.

Ethnic belonging and multiculturalism

Since the emergence of popular sovereignty and its concomitant ideology of nationalism, the operative principle of modern political life has been that the nation-state ought to have a single public identity to which all its citizenry subscribe. Such cohesiveness is regularly credited for maintaining political stability – and its absence is often construed as an indication of potential conflict and fragmentation (Horowitz 1985; Snyder 2000). To put it most crudely, from this perspective uniformity in public life is 'good' and plurality in public life is 'bad'.

Accordingly, public discourse within nation-states tends to be deliberately homogenizing – assimilating, suppressing, denying or excluding alternative and thus potentially rival identifications, including those ethnic attachments which are inconsistent with the state's official persona. Empires could be plural not only sociologically (as Furnivall described them) but even constitutionally (as outlined by Martin Wight) precisely because in this context the right to rule was not constructed in terms of a popular consent conferred from below (the people) but rather a fiduciary responsibility justified from above (i.e., by reference to European civilization and western legal norms). In contrast, while nation-states are usually sociologically plural, with a few notable exceptions (Switzerland, Belgium and Canada, for example) their constitutional arrangements have tended to recognize only one nation or constituent people (as in France, Greece, Turkey, Kenya, Japan, Chile, etc.).

Recently, however, this prejudice in favour of homogeneity in public life has been challenged on both normative and pragmatic grounds. The essential idea behind multiculturalism as developed by Will Kymlicka, Charles Taylor, Joseph Raz, Judith Shklar and like-minded political theorists is that political integration should not be equated with cultural homogenization but should instead seek to recognize the cultural distinctiveness of all members of society while ensuring that they also possess equal citizenship and protection from discrimination (Gutman 1994; Kymlicka 1995). Multicultural theorists argue that such policies are to be preferred not only because they are more likely to encourage minority acceptance of the existing political community and thus support rather than subvert stability but also because it is only in situations of social diversity that individual freedom can be fully realized (Berlin 1990; Raz 1986; Shklar 1986).

From the multicultural perspective, ethnic identification and association is not only driven by fate (descent) but also by choice (consent). We cannot choose our ethnicity but we can choose to suppress or express it in our social relations – and it is precisely that element of choice which makes ethnicity a legitimate subject for public policy. In ethnically plural societies, some individuals are inclined to publicly express their ethnic identities but that choice has not always been easy to make because of governmental interference in favour of the dominant ethnicity or even governmental indifference when this is accompanied by a hostile majority opinion. In such circumstances, the choice to express a minority identity will only be made by exceptional individuals who possess the necessary courage and determination to go against official doctrine and majority views. People lacking these robust dispositions are likely to suppress their minority identities and in so doing will, in effect, be denied an important element of freedom.

Such a state of affairs is not only unjust but also potentially destructive of peace and stability. A state which encouraged or even merely turned a blind eye to hostility directed at minority identities would risk undermining its own legitimacy. Individuals who were despised as a result of their race, ethnicity, religion or language, for example, would have serious grievances against the state which allowed such (mis)treatment. Why should individuals support and obey a state which participated or acquiesced in a diminution of their liberty? Why should they pay taxes or serve in the armed forces or in other ways be responsible citizens if that were the case? In short, why should disesteemed people be loyal citizens when their adversity or oppression is encouraged or ignored by public officials? In extreme circumstances, such individuals might even consider themselves justified in taking up arms against the state in defence of their minority community. This is precisely the argument which multicultural theorists direct against those who continue to insist that homogeneity in public affairs is to be preferred over the recognition of diversity in the interest of peace and democratic government (where this is defined in terms of majority rule).

Multicultural states are imagined as communities of consent and not of descent. But unlike the civic nation-state which relegates ethnicity to the private sphere, the multicultural state publicly recognizes and affirms the diverse ethnic, religious and linguistic identities of its citizens. This public recognition may take different forms: it might consist of the recognition of special rights over and above those of equal citizenship intended to help preserve and promote minority identities; or it could take the form of governmental structures (federalism, autonomy, power-sharing, proportional representation) designed to encourage more effective minority participation in public life; or it might include educational and cultural policies designed to encourage public awareness and understanding of minority identities; or some combination thereof. Whatever its form, however, the key difference between a multicultural state and a traditional nation-state of either the civic or the ethnic type is its inclusion of minority identities within official public discourse.

The challenge in all of this, of course, is to ensure that a minimum of common public values are shared across all social groups, not least of which being that respect for difference without which multiculturalism could not exist. Multiculturalism does not aspire to the creation of so many ethnic solitudes but instead an inclusive conversation which crosses ethnic and other divides. Nor should it be confused with cultural relativism since it continues to place a premium on certain values. At the end of the day, most (liberal) multicultural theorists will choose individual freedom over and above group rights where the two conflict.

Sandra Lovelace v. Canada is a classic illustration of just such a clash of values. Sandra Lovelace was born and registered a 'Maliseet Indian' but lost her rights and status as an Indian under section 12(1)(b) of Canada's Indian Act (1876) after she married a non-Indian. The Supreme Court of Canada had already ruled – in *The Attorney-General of Canada v. Jeanette Lavalle* and in *Richard Isaac et al. v. Ivonne Bedard* – that section 12(1)(b) was fully operative irrespective of its inconsistency with the Canadian Bill of Rights gender equality provisions. Consequently, Lovelace used her individual right of petition under the Optional Protocol of the ICCPR to appeal to the UN Human Rights Committee.

In defence of its position, the Canadian government argued that the Indian Act (1876) was designed to protect the Indian minority in accordance with article 27 of the ICCPR.

> A definition of the Indian was inevitable in view of the special privileges granted to the Indian communities, in particular their right to occupy reserve lands. Traditionally, patrilineal family relationships were taken into account for determining legal claims. Since, additionally, in the farming societies of the nineteenth century, reserve land was felt to be more threatened by non-Indian men than by non-Indian women, legal enactments as from 1869 provided that an Indian woman who married a non-Indian man would lose her status as an Indian. These reasons [are] still valid. A change in the law could only be sought in consultation with the Indians themselves who, however, [are] divided on the issue of equal rights. The Indian community should not be endangered by legislative changes. (United Nations 1981: paragraph 5)

Nevertheless, the Committee found in favour of Lovelace on the grounds that statutory restrictions affecting the right to residence on a reserve of a person belonging to the minority concerned 'must have both a reasonable and objective justification and be consistent with the other provisions of the Covenant', most notably those provisions relating to gender equality (United Nations 1981: paragraph 16). Subsequently, Canada's Indian Act (1876) was amended (in 1985) to restore status to people who had lost it as a result of marrying a man who was not a 'Status Indian'.

Ethnic belonging between communities

It is also as a consequence of the doctrine of popular sovereignty that questions of ethnic belonging entered into relations between communities. Accordingly, from the late eighteenth century onwards, international affairs were no longer the exclusive preserve of sovereign princes and their dynastic ambitions. Instead, a new language of diplomacy and statecraft began to emerge in which the national interest of the population within states became an ever more important point of reference. We see this already in Napoleon's attempts to rearrange the map of Europe along national lines in the final years of the eighteenth century and the beginning of the nineteenth. Although Napoleon's ambitions had rather more in common with dynasts like Henry VIII or Louis XIV than they did with national figures such as James Madison or Maximilien Robespierre, his tactics nevertheless reflected an awareness of the power of popular sentiment, including ethnic attachments. Accordingly, he appealed directly to the populations within dynastic states, offering them a certain degree of national autonomy if they agreed to join the expanding Napoleonic empire (Jackson Preece 1998b: 58–9).

While Napoleon was eventually defeated at Waterloo in 1815, Europe and ultimately also the rest of the world was nevertheless destined for a long period of unrest that efforts to hold back the tide of nationalism did little, if anything, to prevent.

> The victors [who defeated Napoleon] did their best to ensure that the settlement they devised [outlined in the 1815 Final Act of the Congress of Vienna] would be lasting, but the turmoil bequeathed from revolutionary and Napoleonic times, the inexorable social changes, acting separately or jointly, always threatened, and in the end overthrew the 1815 settlement. Those who opposed it did so on the ground that it took no account of the wishes of the peoples [as, for instance, when mainly Catholic Belgium was unified with mainly Protestant Holland], and that rulers were imposed on subjects who had not been consulted [which held true for all the territorial readjustments], and that territories which were naturally one were artificially separated [the most notorious example being the partition of Poland between the Kingdom of Prussia, the Hapsburg Empire, and the Russian Empire]. The two grievances were entwined with each other, both of them indeed the outcome of philosophical speculations which had preceded and accompanied the French Revolution. (Kedourie 1960: 96)

Thus, despite attempts to preserve the dynastic states system, the nineteenth century witnessed a steady growth in the number of nation-states as more and more European peoples successfully claimed for themselves that right (sovereignty) which had hitherto been the birthright of princes: Belgium (after a war of independence against Holland) in 1830; Greece (after a war of independence against the Ottoman Empire) in

1830; Italy (unified by Garibaldi's defeat of the Bourbons) in 1861; Germany (unified after victory over Denmark in 1864 and France in 1870–1) in 1871; and Serbia, Montenegro and Romania (after victory against the Ottoman Empire in the Russo-Turkish War of 1877–8) in 1878.

The passage from Kedourie is significant because it captures a dynamic which continues to characterize the effects of nationalism on international society. From roughly 1815, there arose and has continued to exist within international relations a tension between the aspirations of popular sentiment (defined in no small part by ethnic affinities) and the requirements of political stability (defined in terms of the existing territorial status quo). Such a dynamic goes to the very foundations of international society because it has the potential to pit the two cornerstones of statehood – territory and population – against one another.

Consequently, international society has assumed a contradictory stance towards ethnic diversity depending upon the level – state or sub-state – at which it exists. On the one hand, international society seeks to preserve that ethnic diversity reflected in its plural state membership. At the same time, however, there is a tendency to control or suppress ethnic diversity within states which threatens to disrupt or destabilize international order defined as the continued existence of international society as a whole – although not necessarily the independence of particular states (Bull 1977: 16–17). This Janus-faced response to ethnic diversity is nowhere more readily apparent than in the international history of self-determination.

National self-determination

The idea of national self-determination may be traced back to Woodrow Wilson's vision of a post-World War I peace. The creation of nation-states in the territories of the defeated and discredited Habsburg and Ottoman empires was a major component of his plan: accordingly, a dozen new or enlarged states in Central and Eastern Europe were admitted to international society during the interwar period – these include Austria, Hungary, Poland, Czechoslovakia, Romania,

Bulgaria, the Kingdom of Serbs, Croats and Slovenes (later renamed Yugoslavia), Greece, Albania, Estonia, Latvia and Lithuania. However, a fundamental weakness in Wilson's ideas for restructuring international society was his failure to realize how indeterminate a criterion national identity was and what little assistance it could actually give in delineating frontiers. As already indicated, the nation can be interpreted in accordance with either civic or ethnic criteria – with very different results. If nations are defined by shared political institutions and common citizenship rights within inherited jurisdictions (*jus solis*), then anomalous ethnic communities are, in principle at least, less problematic; if nations are defined by ethnicity, language and culture within historic homelands (*jus sanguinis*), then ethnic diversity is deeply controversial.

The methods used to define nation-states in 1919 were contradictory. Plebiscites evocative of the civic tradition were employed while at the same time ethnographic and linguistic evidence suggestive of the ethnic tradition were also taken into account. On certain occasions decisions were made on the basis of *realpolitik* and even punitive justice – as for example in the incorporation of majority ethnic German Sudetenland within Czechoslovakia (despite Sudeten German requests for assignment to Austria) and the gift of majority ethnic Hungarian Transylvania to Romania. Once it became clear that not all claims to self-determination could or would be recognized in the 1919 territorial settlement, the potential for ethnic dissatisfaction with the territorial status quo to escalate into domestic and even international violence was obvious.

During the interwar period, there were two distinct albeit related international responses to this dilemma: population transfer agreements and international minority rights guarantees. Both of these ideas reflect the then widespread assumption that, wherever possible, ethnic homogeneity within states was to be preferred to diversity in the interests of international peace and stability. Similarly, where homogeneity was not immediately obtainable, it was thought that international supervision and collective security measures could be used to encourage group coexistence and thus prevent ethnic conflicts from destabilizing that territorial status quo on which the new international system was based.

Population transfer (the movement, sometimes forcible, of minorities between states) was viewed as a legitimate means of improving the fit between international boundaries and the ethnic composition of the population within them. National minorities who remained outside the boundaries of their ethnic group's nation-state could simply be relocated. It was hoped this would ease tensions both within and between states by reducing the incidence of disruptive minority claims for self-determination. At the same time, the transfer of minorities to their ethnic group's nation-state was considered the fulfilment of that minority's right to self-determination – once moved, they would become a part of that body politic which reflected their particular ethnicity. This position was endorsed in the 1923 Treaty of Lausanne which authorized and (in theory) regulated the transfer of populations between Greece and Turkey. As a result of this treaty, the respective minorities were either forced to leave Greece or Turkey or – having fled during the war of 1922 – were prohibited from returning. Although many of the treaty's provisions ultimately proved unworkable (especially those guaranteeing compensation for properties left behind), Lausanne nevertheless became an oft-cited precedent for transfers of population throughout the 1920s, 1930s and 1940s (Jackson Preece 1998a: 824–5).

In circumstances where population transfers either could not be used, or were considered undesirable, provisions were made for internationally supervised minority guarantees. The interwar minority rights system was based upon a series of treaties which linked the recognition of new or enlarged states in Central and Eastern Europe, the Baltics and, exceptionally, also Iraq with undertakings to protect ethnic minorities. Such treaties were then placed under the guarantee of the League of Nations. In theory, this legalistic procedure was designed to ensure compliance through a combination of collective decision making and the moral approbation of international public opinion. In practice, however, this consensual conflict resolution formula broke down because the international good will it relied upon was not forthcoming. As a result, minority questions degenerated into a political struggle between, on the one hand, minorities and kin-states with revisionist aims towards the international boundaries set by the treaties of 1919 and, on the other hand, those treaty-bound states that wished to preserve the territorial status quo where it was to their advantage: Germany versus Poland; Germany versus Czechoslovakia; Poland versus Lithuania; Hungary versus Romania; Austria versus Yugoslavia; Bulgaria versus Greece; Greece versus Turkey; and Greece versus Albania. Consequently, and ironically, the League of Nations System of Minority Guarantees – with few exceptions – satisfied neither the minorities it was intended to protect nor the states on which it was imposed (Jackson Preece 1998b: 67–95).

Self-determination of peoples

After 1945, the United Nations was reluctant to adopt the interwar rhetoric of national self-determination and its con-comitant language of national minority rights. Inis Claude contends that the 1945 Charter of the United Nations was for-mulated 'without consideration of the questions of principle' which arise from the existence of national minorities in a 'world dominated by the concept of the national State as the . . . unit of political organization' (Claude 1955: 113). More than this, however, there was a deliberate move to discredit the idea of self-determination understood in ethnic terms. This was in large measure a reaction against the failure of the League experiment and indeed the 1919 system of nation-states and national self-determination which underscored it.

Understandably in the aftermath of World War II, national self-determination – and the secession and irredentism it could provoke – were viewed as serious would-be threats to interna-tional order. Such fears were only heightened by the prospect of widespread decolonization and the creation of new, and potentially weak, states in Asia and Africa. As a result, the UN Charter incorporates the vague phrase 'self-determination of peoples' as distinct from the more familiar and discredited 'national self-determination' in the hope of avoiding that sort of minority controversy which had plagued the League of Nations system. Articles 73 and 76 further define such 'peoples' in terms of the pre-existing colonial territory and not according to ethnicity. The use of civic criteria for assessing claims to self-determination was clearly motivated by a desire to preserve the colonial territorial status quo and in so doing international peace and stability. This position was specifically expressed and affirmed in the 1960 UN Declaration on the Granting of Independence to Colonial Countries and Peoples, which clearly states that 'any attempt aimed at the partial or total disruption of the national unity or territorial integrity of a country is incompatible with the purposes and principles of the United Nations Charter'.

The international legitimization of pre-existing territorial units remains a fundamental practice of international society. Thus, while Czechoslovakia, Yugoslavia and the Soviet Union were replaced by successor states in the 1990s, the new boundaries follow those of the defunct domestic political structures as per the (public international law) principle of *uti possidetis juris* (derived from the Roman legal principle *uti possidetis, ita possideatis* or 'as you possess, so may you possess'). Just as with decolonization in Latin America, Asia and Africa, internal boundaries were inherited without regard to ethnic demographics. Consequently, regions which were not highest level constituent units of the old polities – e.g., Kosovo within Yugoslavia or Chechnya within the Soviet Union – were not entitled to sovereignty despite their distinct ethnic populations and remain as ethnic minority enclaves in the successor states of Serbia-Montenegro and Russia respectively. Such an interpretation is directly aimed at preventing further fragmentation and the additional political instability that might unleash. Territorial integrity determines which claims to independence will take priority and so order continues to trump self-determination except where the states involved so agree (as in the Czechoslovak 'velvet divorce').

To the extent that international society maintains a global states system, it facilitates the political expression of a diverse range of ethnic and other identities: but it is much less able to accommodate that ethnic diversity which remains at the sub-state level because such measures might threaten the territorial integrity and political stability of existing states – and by extension international order itself, which is based on territories not peoples. In those circumstances where a hard choice between competing norms of self-determination for sub-state groups and the sovereignty and territorial integrity of existing states is required, the members of international society will almost always choose the latter. The only exception to this rule applies to those circumstances where the sacrifice of one state is considered necessary to preserve stability within the society of states, as arguably happened when the breakaway Yugoslav republics were recognized as independent states, and again when the 1995 Dayton Agreement created that strange entity known as Republika Serpska within the territory of Bosnia-Herzegovina.

Ethnicity and human rights

The human rights discourse is not intended to promote the rights of ethnic communities and their members but instead the rights of individuals as humans. The great achievement of what we might term the human ethic – as embodied since 1945 not only in human rights but also in humanitarian law and crimes against humanity – is that it has created a normative discourse in which those who abuse their power, regardless of who or where they are, may be condemned. The fact that no government is now willing to admit that its domestic policy aims at the denigration of human rights suggests that these developments are significant even if the problem of enforcement remains owing to the still prevailing condition of international anarchy.

Yet despite its many laudable achievements in championing the rights of oppressed individuals wherever they might be, the human rights perspective is arguably less well suited to dealing with problems of ethnic or indeed other forms of diversity.

> The problem with the concept of human rights is not that it gives the wrong answer to such [minority] questions. It is, rather, that it often gives no answer at all. The right to freedom of speech, for example, does not tell us what language policy a society ought to have. The principles of human rights leave such matters to majoritarian decision-making, and this may result in minorities being vulnerable to injustice at the hands of majorities. Human rights may even make injustice [directed at minorities] worse. (Freeman 2002: 117)

Indeed, there is a tendency for the proponents of human rights to promote civil and political rights (compatible with domestic policies of assimilation) over those cultural rights which would perpetuate ethnic diversity within states. This tendency can be seen in the failure, until very recently, to include measures aimed at the preservation of minority languages, cultures, identities and ways of life alongside equality and anti-discrimination guarantees within international human rights texts.

Until 1992, there was no international instrument devoted exclusively to minority concerns. The only specific mention of minority rights to identity and culture as distinct from equality provisions prior to this time was in article 27 of the 1966 International Covenant on Civil and Political Rights (ICCPR). Article 27 stipulates that 'in those states in which ethnic, religious or linguistic minorities exist, persons belonging to such minorities shall not be denied the right, in community with other members of their group, to enjoy their own culture, to profess and practise their own religion, or to use their own language'. This formulation, however, has been criticized as a minimal guarantee not least because it gives state signatories the freedom to determine whether or not ethnic groups in their jurisdictions constitute minorities. This contrasts with the generous provision for equality guarantees at the United Nations and within many regional organizations, including the Council of Europe, the Organization for Security and Cooperation in Europe (OSCE), the Commonwealth of Nations, the Organization of American States and the African Union.

This general antipathy towards those cultural guarantees which would have recognized and in so doing perpetuated ethnic minorities within existing states is also apparent in the activities of most regional organizations during the period 1945–89. For example, colonial successor states in Latin America, Africa and Asia generally assumed that the absence of minority rights was more conducive to state success defined in terms of territorial integrity and internal political stability than would be the reverse. Thus while the American Convention on Human Rights (1969) reiterates almost all of the rights included in the ICCPR it does not include any reference whatsoever to minority rights along the lines of article 27. This absence of explicit minority provisions is also apparent in the Additional Protocol to the American

Convention on Human Rights in the Area of Economic, Social and Cultural Rights ('Protocol of San Salvador', 1988). Similarly, while the African Charter on Human and Peoples' Rights (1981) incorporates a people's right to self-determination, in practice 'people' has been identified with the already existing African states and not the various tribal groups within them.

Even within Europe, where international minority rights had been recognized under the League System, there was no revival of multilateral guarantees for ethnic minorities between 1945 and 1989 due to the widespread fear that this might rekindle old ethnic conflicts. For example, the Council of Europe – which during this time created what is arguably the most successful regional human rights system in the world – was nonetheless extremely hesitant to pursue a specific minority rights protocol to the European Convention on Human Rights (1950). Instead, it maintained a publicly avowed position that special minority rights were at best 'not very convincing' and at worse 'aggravated existing tensions and difficulties' (Council of Europe 1959). Moreover, minority issues were 'not deemed to be of extreme urgency' because of a widespread belief that protection against discrimination adequately protected all legitimate minority interests (Council of Europe 1961).

And although the Helsinki Final Act (which established the Conference on Security and Cooperation in Europe, precursor to the OSCE) specifically mentions minorities in three different parts of the document – the Declaration on Principles, Principle VII, and the section entitled Cooperation in Humanitarian and Other Fields – the content of the provisions is confined to anti-discrimination measures and allows states a wide latitude in interpreting the kinds of actions that could and could not be undertaken with regard to minorities. Moreover, this initial interest in minority issues was not sustained in the various 'CSCE follow-up meetings' which took place between 1975 and 1989. Instead, these meetings were dominated by a concern for the violation of individual human rights – particularly those civil and political liberties associated with the movement towards human rights and democracy in communist states (Mastney 1992: 11–21). So once again, 'legitimate' minority interests did not include any rights in cultural, educational, religious and linguistic matters over and above those of equal citizenship.

In sum, the circumstances of ethnic and other minorities were largely ignored by international actors during the Cold War due to the widespread conviction that the continued existence of such groups posed a threat to the territorial integrity and social cohesion of existing states and thus also to order and stability within the states system. The only legitimate minority grievances were those concerning problems of individual equality and so international human rights texts from this period give considerable emphasis to equal rights and anti-discrimination provisions but are virtually silent with regard to the special rights over and above equal citizenship necessary to preserve and promote distinct ethnic identities and ways of life.

This international attitude towards ethnic minorities had a number of consequences. It led to the conclusion that such minority matters were not properly subjects of international organizations or multilateral agreements. Instead, and not surprisingly, these issues were understood to be the preserve of the sovereign state in which they occurred. Without international stipulations to the contrary, very many states thus chose to 'resolve' their ethnic minority problems through policies of assimilation or oppression. Unfortunately, as we have recently discovered, the long-term consequences of such policies are very often fundamentally destabilizing for the state affected. Instead of producing a shared identity, the unintended result of assimilation is often a growing minority/majority distrust and antipathy. Similarly, instead of perpetuating the current regime and its underlying ethnic power relations, oppression can provoke violent intercommunal conflicts of the sort recently witnessed, for example, in Rwanda and former Yugoslavia. Thus, ironically, the Cold War stance with regard to ethnic minorities not only failed to protect the interests of these minority communities but very often also failed to preserve the internal stability of the states in which they, however tenuously, existed. But arguably that was a price international society was willing to pay for the sake of overall international order.

The rights of ethnic minorities

The 'problem of ethnic minorities'

Both the civic nation-state and international society tend to subsume ethnicity within the private sphere; as a result, they are often ill-disposed towards the public recognition of diversity except where this is absolutely necessary to preserve social cohesion. The ethnic nation-state incorporates ethnic and similar ascriptive characteristics into the very foundation of its public existence; consequently, it publicly recognizes one ethnic identity while deliberately excluding (often forcibly) any others which might exist within its jurisdiction. And while the idea of a universal humanity confers equal dignity on all individuals, in so doing it tends to downplay and in some instances even ignore ethnic and cultural distinctions regardless of whether or not these are valued.

The normative predicament of ethnic minorities in circumstances where diversity is considered undesirable implies much more than the loss of universal human rights: it involves the loss of specific rights; the loss of a cherished identity; the loss of membership in a particular community in which that identity is recognized and affirmed; the loss of a place in which they can feel fully and completely at home; the loss of meaningful belonging.

> Something much more fundamental than freedom and justice ... is at stake when belonging to the community into which one is born is no longer a matter of course and not belonging no longer a matter of choice ... Not the loss of specific rights, then, but the loss of a community willing and able to guarantee any rights whatsoever, has been the calamity which has befallen ever-increasing numbers of people. (Arendt 1972: 296–7)

The minority rights response

The minority rights response aims to protect and promote the identity and culture of ethnic communities while also protecting the freedom of their individual members. This position is broadly comparable to domestic arrangements for multiculturalism espoused by theorists such as Will Kymlicka, Joseph

Raz and Judith Shklar. In each case, ethnic diversity within states is regarded as the consequence of a political desire for territorial inviolability in the context of a normal human propensity for belonging that makes sociological pluralism a usual and indeed normatively desirable state of affairs. Accordingly, ethnic minorities are not considered to be a prima facie threat to the prevailing social and political order at either the domestic or international level. Instead, the main premise is that minorities who are recognized and supported by the state, and by extension international society, are far less likely to challenge existing modes of authority. Although of relatively recent origin, the minority rights discourse is nevertheless emerging as an increasingly persuasive voice within both domestic and international politics. Since 1989, the hitherto dominant response to ethnic diversity within states (territorial inviolability coupled with individual equality guarantees) has come under growing criticism, not least owing to the increasing incidence of ethnic conflict around the globe. Ironically, that tendency may have strengthened the minority rights position; in this changed world order, the old fear that recognizing minorities might precipitate ethnic violence has now become a moot point. Consequently, a growing list of minority rights, including inter alia provisions for identity, culture, language, participation and a limited degree of self-government, have now been recognized within international standard-setting documents: examples of such provisions may be found in the UN Declaration on the Rights of Persons Belonging to National or Ethnic, Religious and Linguistic Minorities (1992), the European Charter for Regional or Minority Languages (1992) and the Framework Convention for the Protection of National Minorities (1995).

The right to be different

A core component of the minority rights response to ethnic diversity is the public recognition of difference. The idea of recognition includes the right to publicly express one's distinct identity without fear of assimilation, discrimination or persecution. As the UN Declaration on the Rights of Persons Belonging to Minorities puts it: 'States shall protect the existence and the national or ethnic, cultural, religious and linguistic identity of minorities within their respective territories and shall encourage conditions for the promotion of that identity' (article 1(1)). Following on from this, the declaration also affirms that 'Persons belonging to . . . minorities . . . have the right to enjoy their own culture, to profess and practise their own religion, and to use their own language, in private and in public, freely and without interference or any form of discrimination' (article 2(1)). The right to be different can be found in all the main standard setting texts of relevance to the circumstances of ethnic minorities – these include in addition to the UN Declaration on Minorities: article 27 of the ICCPR; articles 5 and 6 of the (European) Framework Convention for the Protection of National Minorities; and articles 3, 4 and 5 of ILO Convention No. 169 Concerning Indigenous and Tribal Peoples in Independent Countries. Although the phraseology and scope of protection varies somewhat from text to text, the basic aim of recognizing diversity remains the same.

The goal of such provisions is to ensure that persons belonging to minorities have the freedom and security to go about their daily business in a manner consistent with their chosen way of life. Accordingly, states must do more than simply demonstrate that there are no express legal prohibitions or penalties to such displays of ethnic difference. They must also ensure that majority public opinion is reasonably sympathetic towards such action on the part of minorities – hence the requirement to 'encourage conditions for the promotion of . . . [ethnic] identity'. Only in such circumstances of minimal respect for diversity can the right to be different fully apply.

The right to participate in public life as a minority

More recently, the basic right to be different has been augmented by a minority right to participate in public life. The ICCPR (1966) contains a broad range of democratic guarantees but makes no mention of a minority right to participation. In contrast, the UN Declaration on Minorities (1992) includes not only a general minority right to 'participate effectively in cultural, religious, social, economic and public life' (article

2(2)) but also a more specific minority right to 'participate effectively in decisions on the national and, where appropriate, regional level concerning the minority to which they belong' (article 2(3)). Participation is of course a requirement of democratic government and the concern that persons belonging to minorities may not be able to participate effectively in representative institutions of this kind has a long history in democratic theory which may be traced back to the nineteenth century writings of John Stuart Mill. However, the usual conclusion following on from this concern has been to advocate minority assimilation as a prerequisite for effective individual participation – thus individuals are ensured their right to participate but in their guise as equal citizens rather than as persons belonging to minorities. Articles 2(2) and 2(3) of the UN Declaration on Minorities as well as article 15 of the (European) Framework Convention are noteworthy as attempts to encourage participation while also respecting the minority right to be different.

The form that effective participation may take will undoubtedly vary from state to state. Nevertheless, certain key attributes of and instruments for participation stand out and one would expect to see at least some of these where minorities are included in the democratic process along the lines envisioned by the leading minority rights documents. The Explanatory Report which accompanies the OSCE-sponsored Lund Recommendations on the Effective Participation of National Minorities in Public Life observes that the 'essence of participation is involvement' both in terms of 'the opportunity to make substantive contributions to decision-making processes' and in terms of 'the effect of those contributions' (OSCE 1999: paragraph 6). Such participation may be achieved in various ways, for instance by reserving seats for minorities within decision making bodies (by way of quotas, promotions or other measures) or by establishing special bodies to accommodate minority concerns. At the same time, meaningful opportunities to exercise minority rights 'require specific steps to be taken in the public service', including ensuring 'equal access to public service' as articulated in Article 5(c) of the International Convention on the Elimination of All Forms of Racial Discrimination (OSCE 1999: paragraph 6).

The right to self-government

Self-determination understood as a right to form separate states is noticeably absent from the leading minority rights standard-setting documents. That is because international law and practice draws a distinction between the right to self-determination and minority rights. Self-determination is considered to be a collective right belonging to peoples while minority rights are conceptualized as individual rights of persons belonging to minorities, albeit with the added proviso that such rights may be exercised in community with other members. This individual formulation not only protects non-conformist members of minorities from undue interference by the rest of the group, it also acts as an important reminder that minority rights are not analogous to the collective right of peoples to self-determination and thus may not be used in support of minority claims for political independence. This distinction between the collective right of self-determination of peoples and the individual rights of persons belonging to minorities is made with the express intention of ensuring that minority rights do not threaten the sovereignty and territorial integrity of existing states. For that same reason, it has become standard practice for minority rights documents specifically to affirm the sovereignty, territorial integrity and political independence of existing states.

Nevertheless, it has been suggested that new developments directed at national minorities and indigenous peoples may be modifying the substance of self-determination to include internal arrangements for self-government which fall short of separate statehood. For example, Section IV (35) of the OSCE's Copenhagen Document (1990) contains a recommendation for 'appropriate local or autonomous administrations corresponding to the specific historical and territorial circumstances of . . . minorities'. The draft national minorities protocol to the European Convention on Human Rights as proposed by the Parliamentary Assembly of the Council of Europe in 1993 would have gone much further in recognizing a minority right to appropriate local or autonomous authorities or a special status matching their specific historical and territorial situation. The United Nations Draft Declaration on the Rights of Indigenous Peoples (1994) is even more emphatic: article 3 clearly states that 'indigenous peoples have the right to self determination . . . [b]y virtue of that right they freely determine their political status and freely pursue their economic, social and cultural development'.

Arguably, national minorities and indigenous peoples are the subjects of extra provisions like these because they represent special cases within the larger category of ethnic minorities. National minorities and indigenous peoples ordinarily did not choose the state in which they now find themselves but were co-opted by it as a result of discovery, conquest, colonization or the transfer of territory between sovereigns. Unlike immigrants, migrants and refugees who are the result of personal movement across political frontiers, national minorities and indigenous peoples remain within their historic territories while over time new frontiers have formed around them. In both of these cases, additional normative claims for self-government have been put forward due to the historic association of such groups with the territories in which they reside and the involuntary nature of their inclusion within existing political frontiers (Jackson Preece 1998b). The fact that this deep attachment to territory can lead to prolonged and bloody conflict over rival claims of political ownership is an added incentive for political actors to make special arrangements for these groups.

Such proposals go beyond the minority right to participation by advocating that national minorities and indigenous peoples should be able to determine and control the internal governmental structures relevant to their circumstances. In so doing, these provisions recognize rather than deny the self-determination claims of national minorities and indigenous peoples understood as a right of internal self-government but not secession. By distinguishing between (external) self-determination and (internal) self-government, it is hoped that the principle of territorial integrity upon which the post-1945 international order rests will be preserved. It must, however, be stressed that such proposals for an internal right to self-government remain highly controversial. The fear of secession is very real in many countries and international reassurances in favour of territorial integrity may do little to assuage it. Moreover, such international requirements are often perceived as an infringement upon the right of states to determine their own governmental arrangements free from outside interference. This perception is especially powerful in post-colonial states who understandably do not wish to compromise their independence. For this reason, such recommendations exist for the most part in draft form within standard-setting documents which have yet to be adopted (the Draft Minority Rights Protocol to the ECHR, the Draft Declaration on the Rights of Indigenous Peoples) or appear as recommendations rather than stipulations in agreed texts (like the Copenhagen Document).

Conclusion

The politicization of ethnicity in its current guise is a consequence of the emergence of popular sovereignty and its concomitant ideology of nationalism. Once popular identity becomes the locus of political authority, then those minority identifications at odds with the established public persona of the nation-state are perceived as a potential threat to the prevailing social and political order within as well as between communities. The belief that peace and stability requires the preservation of a common public identity is pervasive within both civic and ethnic nation-states and may therefore in either case act as a justification for homogenizing policies directed at ethnic and other minorities. That being said, because ties of 'blood' are intrinsic to communities of putative descent like ethnic nation-states, both public opinion and public policy towards minorities are likely to be most hostile in such circumstances.

The minority rights response offers a potential way out of the nationalist impasse with respect to minorities by rethinking the relationship between diversity and stability. From this perspective, minorities who are recognized and respected by the state – and thus become integrated (but not assimilated) within its public persona – are considered less likely to challenge existing political arrangements. Instead of viewing diversity as a 'threat' which must be contained or, if possible, eliminated, the proponents of minority rights see diversity as a 'value' which should be affirmed and protected. Yet whatever view we adopt, ethnicity is likely to remain a matter of political importance for the foreseeable future – our continued adherence to the doctrine of popular sovereignty ensures that this will be the case whether we imagine ourselves as members of national or multicultural communities.

6
Beyond the 'Problem of Minorities'?

The central claim of this book can be briefly stated: minorities are political outsiders whose very existence challenges the prevailing principle of legitimacy. Consequently, the identity of those persons who constitute a 'minority' changes from one political and historical context to another. But the 'problem of minorities' may occur in any historical period. Nor is it limited to domestic society but extends to international society. This problem can be addressed in one of two ways: either by enforcing conformity or by recognizing diversity. Minority rights are an attempt to do the latter. But can the minority rights response finally overcome the 'problem of minorities'? Or is a permanent solution likely to remain elusive? This concluding chapter will summarize the argument thus far and offer some final reflections on the limits of minority rights.

Diversity and community

A political community is not a 'thing' but a system of rules, procedures and roles conducted by individuals (Benn and Peters 1959: 253). In order to function properly, these rules, procedures and roles must be regarded as legitimate. If they are sustained only by force, the political community is likely to fall apart at the first sign of weakness, as happened to the communist regimes in Eastern Europe during 1989 when it became clear that Soviet military power would be withdrawn. Loyalty to the prevailing principle of legitimacy is therefore essential to preserve order and stability within a political community.

What I have termed belonging does not originate in a procedural requirement that minorities must submit to majorities. It derives from the faithfulness of members to an ideal with which each identifies (Benn and Peters 1959: 244). Otherwise diverse or individual agents by their association with this fundamental normative characteristic become alike or uniform and are accordingly united in this respect (Collingwood 2000: 138–9). What matters is not the content of the ideal but rather its ability to sustain a sense of solidarity towards other members that is not ordinarily extended to outsiders. As we have seen, this ideal can take many different forms – in medieval Christendom, it was an ideal of personal submission to the will of the Christian god; in dynastic states, it was an ideal of personal submission to the will of the sovereign prince; in civic nation-states, it was an ideal of equal citizenship; in ethnic nation-states it was an ideal of cosanguinity; in European overseas empires it was an ideal of (European) 'civilization'; in multicultural states it was an ideal of mutual respect for difference. Collective belonging within a political community is by definition conformist in relation to this essential normative characteristic whatever it might be and so diversity which contradicts or challenges that key characteristic is a potential threat.

In every political community, order and stability is arguably defined in terms of the prevailing principle of legitimacy and its ability to preserve group cohesiveness. It is not diversity per se which is a problem, but only that diversity which contradicts this ideal because in so doing it threatens the basis of political community. Other forms of diversity which have no bearing on this key characteristic are politically irrelevant and therefore may be safely ignored. Medieval Christendom was able to accommodate a wide array of ethnic and linguistic diversity but it could not tolerate religious beliefs which challenged Catholic doctrine; dynastic states could contain ethnic, linguistic and in some cases even religious diversity provided that the will of the sovereign prince was recognized as supreme; the citizens of civic nation-states could be diverse in their private language, religion, ethnicity and race so long as public institutions and civic values were not compromised; ethnic nation-states are least able to accommodate diversity because of the emphasis on cosanguinity but even in such circumstances some characteristics may be less significant than others (as in Germany where historically language and later race defined ethnicity but not religion so that Germans could be either Catholic or Protestant); European overseas empires were quite obviously diverse in religion, race, language and ethnicity but they nevertheless privileged (European) civilization; and multicultural states champion the ideal of respect for difference but as a result cannot tolerate who and what they define as intolerant.

Enforcing conformity

One way of resolving the 'problem of minorities' is to enforce conformity with whatever ideal legitimates a political community. Such enforcement can take several different forms, which may be grouped into four broad categories: discrimination; assimilation; persecution; or separation. These categories are not exclusive and may in fact be mutually reinforcing.

Discrimination involves singling out those who are different from whatever ideal sustains a community and limiting their access to and enjoyment of the benefits of membership. Minorities may, for example, find their educational and occupational choices limited, their freedom to live and work in certain areas curtailed, their ability to purchase, inherit or otherwise own property restricted and their participation in community institutions denied. We find practices like these directed at the Jewish population of medieval Christendom, the Catholic population of England prior to emancipation in 1829, as well as the black population of the so-called 'Jim Crow' states of America before the 1964 US Civil Rights Act. Discrimination is intended to make it difficult for the minority in question to sustain its separate existence and thus encourage the attrition of its members through flight, assimilation or increased mortality.

Through assimilation persons belonging to minorities are absorbed into the larger society, thereby removing all public evidence of diversity. Assimilation may result from social pressure to conform – in which case, persons belonging to minorities adopt the outward trappings of the majority in order to gain acceptance and upward mobility. The so-called 'American melting pot' in which immigrants of diverse origins acquired an American identity is perhaps the most well-known example. Alternatively, assimilation may be directly enforced, in which case persons belonging to minorities are required to speak only the official language, worship only according to the official religion and otherwise cease to conduct their lives in any manner which would distinguish them from the rest of the population. In such circumstances, compliance is generally obtained through punishment (including fines, imprisonment and in some circumstances even death) or expulsion. Such policies were employed by the communist government of Todor Zhivkov against the Turkish minority of Bulgaria between 1984 and 1989. Ethnic Turks were required to change their names to Bulgarian equivalents – often by military officials and at the point of a gun. Those who refused to assimilate lost their jobs, were denied access to education and faced possible imprisonment.

Persecution can include a wide range of actions with varying degrees of violence – it may involve harassment, verbal or physical abuse, or even death. And it can be conducted either by agents or representatives of the political community or by the public at large. As with discrimination, the intention is to disrupt the lives of persons belonging to minorities so that they are encouraged to either flee or assimilate. The inquisitorial system that was designed to seek out and punish heretics within medieval Europe is an infamous example of officially organized persecution, while anti-Semitic violence is perhaps the classic example of spontaneous persecution.

Separation is the most direct method of enforcing conformity. In such circumstances, the minority in question is detached from the rest of the community, which becomes more homogeneous as a result. Separation can take different forms: it may involve legal or administrative division in which the minority is accorded a status distinct from that of the majority, as in the Ottoman millet system; or it may involve the physical removal of the minority into a separate geographical space within the community (i.e., a ghetto) or beyond its frontiers (as in the notorious policy of 'Indian removals' to lands west of the Mississippi) or to another community in which the minority will become the majority (as in the interwar transfer of populations between Greece and Turkey); or, at its most extreme, it may involve the physical annihilation of the minority (i.e., genocide) as a final act of separation.

In each of these scenarios, diversity which challenges the prevailing principle of legitimacy is viewed as a prima facie threat. The political response is thus to eliminate diversity and in so doing overcome the 'problem of minorities'. But history demonstrates that such attempts to enforce conformity are at best temporary and incomplete due to the recalcitrant nature of individual and collective identities and the constant movement of peoples within and indeed across frontiers. Ultimately, human diversity is remarkably resilient. Consequently, in addition to the human suffering they entail, such policies may exacerbate the very minority/majority conflicts they hoped to avoid.

Recognizing diversity

An alternative way of responding to the 'problem of minorities' is to recognize diversity for what it is – not an aberration but the usual state of affairs. Minorities are a direct consequence of our normal human propensity to seek out those who share our values and interests. This explains why minorities are frequently resistant to policies intended to deny or erode their distinctiveness. And it makes the proponents of minority rights believe that minorities who are recognized and supported by the political community will be less likely to challenge its authority or threaten its territorial integrity.

Special guarantees for minorities intended to prevent political instability are not a recent development. As early as the seventeenth century, one finds evidence of such provisions for religious minorities in territories transferred between sovereigns. By the end of the nineteenth century, arrangements like these had become a standard feature of those international treaties which recognized new or enlarged states. In the interwar period, this practice culminated in the League of Nations System of Minority Guarantees which included not only religious but also linguistic and other rights. Even during the Cold War, when multilateral minority rights fell in abeyance, many states continued to manage their diversity dilemmas through domestic and bilateral arrangements to protect minorities, albeit with varying degrees of success: these countries include Austria, Belgium, Canada, Cyprus, Denmark, Fiji, Finland, Germany, Italy, Lebanon, Malaysia, Switzerland and Yugoslavia.

But it is only in the period since 1989 that minority rights have emerged as the 'new orthodoxy' in political thinking about diversity. Since this time political theorists, public policy makers and international lawyers have increasingly come to the conclusion that recognizing diversity as opposed to enforcing conformity is the preferred way of responding to the 'problem of minorities' not only for the sake of order and stability but also out of respect for the minorities themselves. As a result, a growing list of minority rights including inter alia provisions for identity, culture, language, equality, participation and a limited degree of internal self-government have now been recognized within standard-setting documents of various kinds: examples of such provisions may be found in the UN Declaration on the Rights of Persons Belonging to National or Ethnic, Religious and Linguistic Minorities (1992), the European Charter for Regional or Minority Languages (1992), the European Framework Convention for the Protection of National Minorities (1995), the General Framework Agreement for Peace in Bosnia (the 'Dayton Agreement') (1995), the Northern Ireland Peace Agreement (1998), the Bougainville Peace Agreement (2001) and the Constitutional Framework for Provisional Self-Government in Kosovo (2001), among others.

The minority rights response is certainly more sympathetic to the plight of minorities than those policies which seek to enforce conformity. But it should not therefore be assumed that minority rights are able to finally resolve the contradiction between diversity and community. Freedom and belonging remain mutually incommensurate albeit equally compelling ideals: to quote Isaiah Berlin, 'we are doomed to choose and every choice may entail an irreparable loss' (Berlin 1990: 13). Minority rights cannot once and for all overcome the 'problem of minorities' precisely because there is an inherent contradiction between freedom manifested as diversity and belonging manifested as community. The best they can do is provide us with a moral and legal framework in which hard choices can be adjudicated.

Minority rights as a moral and legal framework

A minority rights response to diversity will include legal and quasi-legal provisions which identify specific minority rights holders and accord them substantive guarantees that address their particular circumstances. In so doing, a series of corresponding duties will also be created and compliance procedures (judicial or political, domestic or international) may be identified to ensure these duties are fulfilled. Such provisions may be located at either the domestic or the international level or indeed a combination of the two. And they may be found in different kinds of texts – constitutions, domestic legislation, power-sharing agreements, international treaties and declaratory statements.

As normative entitlements, minority rights are intended to create a lasting series of rules and relationships. Once accepted, they are usually no longer legitimate subjects for political negotiation or compromise and instead are deliberately placed beyond the everyday reach of political actors, in a manner reminiscent of constitutional entrenchment. Generally speaking, rights may only be modified or derogated from in exceptional circumstances and according to stipulated procedures. Similarly, the responsibility of adjudicating between rights is usually assigned to the courts and not the legislature. In this sense, rights trump political interests.

The rights included in the main international standard-setting documents of relevance to minorities – namely the UN Declaration on the Rights of Persons Belonging to Minorities, the UN Convention on the Elimination of All Forms of Racial Discrimination, article 27 of the International Covenant on Civil and Political Rights, the European Framework Convention for the Protection of National Minorities, and the European Charter for Regional or Minority Languages – are all individual entitlements. As such, these provisions recognize the rights of individual persons 'belonging to minorities'. They do not recognize the rights of minority groups per se. Instead, a collective element is achieved only indirectly through the proviso that these individual minority rights may be exercised 'in community with other members'.

The difficulty of balancing between individuals and groups remains a crucial issue. But in practice, there is a reasonably well-established hierarchy within the various minority rights texts that is designed to do precisely that. Where conflicts of rights occur between individuals and groups, moral primacy is usually accorded to the individual as the ultimate source of collective legitimacy. In other words, the normative value assigned to groups is derivative of the more fundamental normative value vested in individuals. Accordingly, groups must respect the autonomy of their individual members including those who freely choose to dissent from majority opinions or ways of life. This will be recognized as a classical liberal approach.

In order to become actualized, rights presuppose rules which are incorporated into everyday social and political life. For example, my right to speak a minority language or to wear traditional dress is meaningless unless the judicial and police systems are prepared to enforce it against those who might otherwise refuse to serve me in stores or restaurants, verbally or physically abuse me or in some other way interfere with my ability to exercise the right in question. This reality underscores the fundamental connection between legal guarantees and political practices. And it necessitates hard choices between competing values and would-be claimants.

Hard choices

Should 'mounties' wear turbans? Should mosques be subject to police searches? Should race be a factor in university admissions? Should women who marry out lose their membership in minority communities? Each of these dilemmas represents a hard choice between equally compelling yet mutually incommensurate values – minority identity versus public identity; freedom of religion versus security; past inequality versus present inequality; minority tradition versus gender equality. Whatever the decision, one value will have to be sacrificed in order to preserve the other.

Even where a minority rights framework exists, there are no easy solutions to such dilemmas. Because the values at stake are incommensurate, there is no straightforward 'right' or 'wrong' answer. Where collisions of values arise we can expect only reasonable choices, not perfect choices. Reasonable choices are the best choices in the circumstances (Jackson 2000: 22). And different circumstances are likely to yield different decisions. In *Grutter v. Bollinger* the US Supreme Court ruled in favour of race as one factor in university admissions, while in *Gratz v. Bollinger* the same court ruled against an admissions system that relied more explicitly on race through a points system. Such apparent inconsistencies are only to be expected when collisions of values occur.

This is not an argument in favour of cultural or moral relativism but normative pluralism: 'the conception that there are many different ends that men may seek and still be fully rational, fully men, capable of understanding each other. . . .' (Berlin 1990: 11). Members of one culture can recognize the values of another culture. They may find these values morally unacceptable but are nevertheless capable of imagining a life dedicated to their fulfilment. Intercultural dialogue is possible because what makes us human is constant across time and space. 'We are free to criticise the values of other cultures, to condemn them, but we cannot pretend not to understand them at all, or to regard them simply as subjective, the products of creatures in different circumstances with different tastes from our own, which do not speak to us at all' (Berlin 1990: 11). As a result, what we are left with is a situational ethic which attempts to balance a respect for diversity against the requirements of community. Hard choices will always arise – the incommensurability of diversity and community makes this unavoidable. But these conflicts can be minimized by promoting and preserving an uneasy equilibrium, albeit one that is constantly endangered and constantly in need of rebalancing – that is what the minority rights response tries to do. The proponents of minority rights hope to ensure that conflicting values are seen as elements in a total way of life that can be enhanced or damaged by political decisions so that all relevant circumstances are taken into account when hard choices must be made. In other words, minority rights aim to give equal consideration to both diversity and community. Such an outcome does not remove the necessity of choosing between diversity and community, but it arguably increases the likelihood that whatever choice is made will be reasonable.

APPENDIX A

Declaration on the Rights of Persons Belonging to National or Ethnic, Religious and Linguistic Minorities

Adopted by General Assembly resolution 47/135 of 18 December 1992

The General Assembly,

Reaffirming that one of the basic aims of the United Nations, as proclaimed in the Charter, is to promote and encourage respect for human rights and for fundamental freedoms for all, without distinction as to race, sex, language or religion,

Reaffirming faith in fundamental human rights, in the dignity and worth of the human person, in the equal rights of men and women and of nations large and small,

Desiring to promote the realization of the principles contained in the Charter, the Universal Declaration of Human Rights, the Convention on the Prevention and Punishment of the Crime of Genocide, the International Convention on the Elimination of All Forms of Racial Discrimination, the International Covenant on Civil and Political Rights, the International Covenant on Economic, Social and Cultural Rights, the Declaration on the Elimination of All Forms of Intolerance and of Discrimination Based on Religion or Belief, and the Convention on the Rights of the Child, as well as other relevant international instruments that have been adopted at the universal or regional level and those concluded between individual States Members of the United Nations,

Inspired by the provisions of article 27 of the International Covenant on Civil and Political Rights concerning the rights of persons belonging to ethnic, religious and linguistic minorities,

Considering that the promotion and protection of the rights of persons belonging to national or ethnic, religious and linguistic minorities contribute to the political and social stability of States in which they live,

Emphasizing that the constant promotion and realization of the rights of persons belonging to national or ethnic, religious and linguistic minorities, as an integral part of the development of society as a whole and within a democratic framework based on the rule of law, would contribute to the strengthening of friendship and cooperation among peoples and States,

Considering that the United Nations has an important role to play regarding the protection of minorities,

Bearing in mind the work done so far within the United Nations system, in particular by the Commission on Human Rights, the Subcommission on Prevention of Discrimination and Protection of Minorities and the bodies established pursuant to the International Covenants on Human Rights and other relevant international human rights instruments in promoting and protecting the rights of persons belonging to national or ethnic, religious and linguistic minorities,

Taking into account the important work which is done by intergovernmental and non-governmental organizations in protecting minorities and in promoting and protecting the rights of persons belonging to national or ethnic, religious and linguistic minorities,

Recognizing the need to ensure even more effective implementation of international human rights instruments with regard to the rights of persons belonging to national or ethnic, religious and linguistic minorities,

Proclaims this Declaration on the Rights of Persons Belonging to National or Ethnic, Religious and Linguistic Minorities:

Article 1

1. States shall protect the existence and the national or ethnic, cultural, religious and linguistic identity of minorities within their respective territories and shall encourage conditions for the promotion of that identity.

2. States shall adopt appropriate legislative and other measures to achieve those ends.

Article 2

1. Persons belonging to national or ethnic, religious and linguistic minorities (hereinafter referred to as persons belonging to minorities) have the right to enjoy their own culture, to profess and practise their own religion, and to use their own language, in private and in public, freely and without interference or any form of discrimination.

2. Persons belonging to minorities have the right to participate effectively in cultural, religious, social, economic and public life.

3. Persons belonging to minorities have the right to participate effectively in decisions on the national and, where appropriate, regional level concerning the minority to which they belong or the regions in which they live, in a manner not incompatible with national legislation.

4. Persons belonging to minorities have the right to establish and maintain their own associations.

5. Persons belonging to minorities have the right to establish and maintain, without any discrimination, free and peaceful contacts with other members of their group and with persons belonging to other minorities, as well as contacts across frontiers with citizens of other States to whom they are related by national or ethnic, religious or linguistic ties.

Article 3

1. Persons belonging to minorities may exercise their rights, including those set forth in the present Declaration, individually as well as in community with other members of their group, without any discrimination.

2. No disadvantage shall result for any person belonging to a minority as the consequence of the exercise or non-exercise of the rights set forth in the present Declaration.

Article 4

1. States shall take measures where required to ensure that persons belonging to minorities may exercise fully and effectively all their human rights and fundamental freedoms without any discrimination and in full equality before the law.

2. States shall take measures to create favourable conditions to enable persons belonging to minorities to express their characteristics and to develop their culture, language, religion, traditions and customs, except where specific practices are in violation of national law and contrary to international standards.

3. States should take appropriate measures so that, wherever possible, persons belonging to minorities may have adequate opportunities to learn their mother tongue or to have instruction in their mother tongue.

4. States should, where appropriate, take measures in the field of education, in order to encourage knowledge of the history, traditions, language and culture of the minorities existing within their territory.

Persons belonging to minorities should have adequate opportunities to gain knowledge of the society as a whole.

5. States should consider appropriate measures so that persons belonging to minorities may participate fully in the economic progress and development in their country.

Article 5

1. National policies and programmes shall be planned and implemented with due regard for the legitimate interests of persons belonging to minorities.

2. Programmes of cooperation and assistance among States should be planned and implemented with due regard for the legitimate interests of persons belonging to minorities.

Article 6

States should cooperate on questions relating to persons belonging to minorities, inter alia, exchanging information and experiences, in order to promote mutual understanding and confidence.

Article 7

States should cooperate in order to promote respect for the rights set forth in the present Declaration.

Article 8

1. Nothing in the present Declaration shall prevent the fulfilment of international obligations of States in relation to persons belonging to minorities. In particular, States shall fulfil in good faith the obligations and commitments they have assumed under international treaties and agreements to which they are parties.

2. The exercise of the rights set forth in the present Declaration shall not prejudice the enjoyment by all persons of universally recognized human rights and fundamental freedoms.

3. Measures taken by States to ensure the effective enjoyment of the rights set forth in the present Declaration shall not prima facie be considered contrary to the principle of equality contained in the Universal Declaration of Human Rights.

4. Nothing in the present Declaration may be construed as permitting any activity contrary to the purposes and principles of the United

Nations, including sovereign equality, territorial integrity and political independence of States.

Article 9

The specialized agencies and other organizations of the United Nations system shall contribute to the full realization of the rights and principles set forth in the present Declaration, within their respective fields of competence.

APPENDIX B
Selected Documents

Global

Universal Declaration of Human Rights (UDHR) (1948)
www.unhchr. ch/udhr/index.htm

Convention on the Prevention and Punishment of the Crime of Genocide
(1948) www.unhchr.ch/html/menu3/b/p_genoci.htm

UN Declaration on the Granting of Independence to Colonial Countries
and Peoples (1960) http://daccessdds.un.org/doc/RESOLUTION/GEN/
NR0/152/88/IMG/NR015288.pdf?OpenElement

International Convention on the Elimination of All Forms of Racial
Discrimination (CERD) (1965) www.ohchr.org/english/law/cerd.htm

International Covenant on Civil and Political Rights (ICCPR) (1966)
www.ohchr.org/english/law/ccpr.htm

Declaration on the Elimination of All Forms of Intolerance and
Discrimination Based on Religion or Belief (DEDR) (1981)
www. unhchr.ch/html/menu3/b/d_intole.htm

ILO Convention (No. 169) Concerning Indigenous and Tribal Peoples
in Independent Countries (1989) www.unhchr.ch/html/menu3/b/62.htm

United Nations Declaration on the Rights of Persons Belonging
to National or Ethnic, Religious and Linguistic Minorities (1992)
www.unhchr.ch/html/menu3/b/d_minori.htm

UN Draft Declaration on the Rights of Indigenous Peoples (1994)
www.unhchr.ch/huridocda/huridoca.nsf/(Symbol)/E.CN.4.SUB.2.RES.
1994.45.En?OpenDocument

Regional

Africa
African Charter on Human and Peoples' Rights ('Banjul Charter')
(1981) www.africa-union.org/Official_documents/Treaties_%20Conve
ntions_%20Protocols/Banjul%20Charter.pdf

Americas
American Convention on Human Rights (ACHR) (1969)
www.oas.org/ juridico/english/Treaties/b-32.htm

Europe
Treaty of Peace with Poland [Polish Minorities Treaty under the League of Nations System of Minority Guarantees] (1919)
www.austlii.edu.au/au/other/dfat/treaties/1920/12.html

European Convention on Human Rights (ECHR) (1950)
www.echr.coe.int/Convention/webConvenENG.pdf

European Charter for Regional or Minority Languages (1992)
http:// conventions.coe.int/treaty/en/Treaties/Html/148.htm

Framework Convention for the Protection of National Minorities (1995) http://conventions.coe.int/treaty/en/Treaties/Html/157.htm

European Union Race Equality Directive (2000) www.equalitytribu nal.ie/htm/equality_legislation_reviews/pdf/RaceDir.pdf

Domestic

Bosnia and Herzegovina
The General Framework Agreement for Peace in Bosnia (Dayton Agreement) (1995) www.ohr.int/dpa/default.asp?content_id=380

Constitution of the Federation of Bosnia and Herzegovina (1997)
www.ohr.int/const/bih-fed/default.asp?content_id=5907

Constitution of Republika Srpska (2001)
www.ohr.int/const/rs/de fault.asp?content_id=5908

Kosovo
Constitutional Agreement for Provisional Self-Government in Kosovo (2001) www.unmikonline.org/constframework.htm

United Kingdom
United Kingdom Race Relations Act (1976)
www.homeoffice.gov.uk/docs/racerel1.html

The Northern Ireland Agreement (1998)
www.nio.gov.uk/agreement.pdf

The Stephen Lawrence Inquiry (1999)
www.archive.official-docume nts.co.uk/docu-ment/cm42/4262/4262.htm#

United States
United States Civil Rights Act (1964)
http://usinfo.state.gov/usa/infousa/laws/majorlaw/civilr19.htm

Plessy v. Ferguson (United States Supreme Court) (1896)
www.land markcases.org/plessy/pdf/plessy_v_ferguson.pdf

Brown v. Board of Education (Supreme Court of the United States)
(1954) www.brownvboard.org/research/opinions/347us483.htm

Loving v. Virginia (Supreme Court of the United States) (1967)
http://supct.law.cornell.edu/supct/html/historics/USSC_CR_0388_0001
_ZO.html

Regents of the University of California v. Bakke (Supreme Court of the
United States) (1978) http://supct.law.cornell.edu/supct/html/historics/
USSC_CR_0438_0265_ZS.html

Gratz v. Bollinger (Supreme Court of the United States) (2003)
http://supct.law.cornell.edu/supct/html/02-516.ZS.html

Grutter v. Bollinger (Supreme Court of the United States) (2003)
http://supct.law.cornell.edu/supct/html/02-241.ZS.html

References

Ackroyd, P. 1998. *The Life of Thomas More.* London: Vintage.

Acton, J. 1907. *The History of Freedom and Other Essays.* London: Macmillan.

Anaya, S. J. 2000. *Indigenous Peoples in International Law.* Oxford: Oxford University Press.

Anderson, B. 1991. *Imagined Communities: Reflections on the Origin and Spread of Nationalism.* London: Verso.

Arendt, H. 1972. *The Origins of Totalitarianism.* New York: World Publishing.

Bailyn, B. 1992. *The Ideological Origins of the American Revolution.* Cambridge, Mass.: Belknap Press.

Bain, W. 2003. *Between Anarchy and Society: Trusteeship and the Obligations of Power.* Oxford: Oxford University Press.

BBC News 2003. Anti-terror Police Raid London Mosque. 20 Jan. 2003. At http://news.bbc.co.uk/2/hi/uk_news/england/2675223.stm.

Beasley, W. 1973. *The Meiji Restoration.* Stanford: Stanford University Press.

Benn, S. and Peters, R. 1959. *Social Principles and the Democratic State.* London: Allen and Unwin.

Berlin, I. 1990. *The Crooked Timber of Humanity: Chapters in the History of Ideas.* London: John Murray.

Bloch M. 1961. *Feudal Society: The Growth of Ties of Dependence,* trans. L. Manyon. London: Routledge.

Boutros-Ghali, B. 1992. *An Agenda for Peace: Preventative Diplomacy, Peacemaking and Peace-Keeping.* A/47/277, New York: United Nations.

Bozeman, A. 1960. *Politics and Culture in International History.* Princeton: Princeton University Press.

Brown, C. 2002. *Sovereignty, Rights and Justice*. Cambridge: Polity.

Brubaker, R. 1992. *Nationalism Reframed: Nationhood and the National Question in the New Europe*. Cambridge: Cambridge University Press.

Bruce, S. 2000. *Fundamentalism*. Cambridge: Polity.

Bull, H. 1977. *The Anarchical Society*. London: Macmillan.

Cameron, E. 1991. *The European Reformation*. Oxford: Oxford University Press.

Catholic Encyclopedia 1908. (New York: Robert Appleton.) Online edition by K. Knight. At www.newadvent.org/cathen/.

Claude, I. 1955. *National Minorities: An International Problem*. Cambridge, Mass.: Harvard University Press.

CNN, 25 December 2003. Narrow Use of Affirmative Action Preserved in College Admissions. At www.cnn.com/2003/LAW/06/23/scotus.affirmative.action/.

Cobban, A. 1970. *The Nation State and National Self-Determination*. New York: Thomas Crowell.

Coffey, J. 2000. *Persecution and Toleration in Protestant England 1558–1689*. Harlow: Pearson Education.

Cohen, W. 2003. *The French Encounter with Africans: White Response to Blacks, 1530–1880*. Bloomington and Indianapolis: Indiana University Press.

Collingwood, R. 2000. *The New Leviathan or Man, Society, Civilization and Barbarism*. Oxford: Clarendon Press.

Council of Europe 1959. *Consultative Assembly Report 1002 on the Position of National Minorities in Europe*.

Council of Europe 1961. *Consultative Assembly Recommendation 285 on the Rights of National Minorities*.

Coupland, R. 1945. *The Durham Report*. Oxford: Clarendon Press.

Daftary, F. and Gal, K. 2003. The 1999 Slovak Minority Language Law: Internal or External Politics? In F. Daftary and F. Grin (eds), *Nation-Building, Ethnicity and Language Politics in Transition Countries*. Budapest: Open Society Institute.

de las Casas, B. 1974. *In Defence of the Indians*, trans. by S. Poole. DeKalb: Northern Illinois University Press.

Dessalines, J. 1804. Declaration of Haitian Independence. At www.geocities.com/ndorestant/independ.htm.

Dilke, C. 1869. *Greater Britain: A Record of Travel in English-Speaking Countries during 1866 and 1867*. New York: Harper.

Donnelly, J. 2003. In Defense of the Universal Declaration Model. In G. Lyons and J. Mayall (eds), *International Human Rights in the Twenty-First Century: Protecting the Rights of Groups*. Oxford: Rowman and Littlefield.

Drumbl, M. 2004. ICTY Appeals Chamber Delivers Two Major Judgments: Blaškić and Krstić. ASIL Insights. At www.asil.org/insights/insigh143.htm.

Emerson, R. 1962. *From Empire to Nation: The Rise to Self-Assertion of Asian and African Peoples.* Cambridge, Mass.: Harvard University Press.

Encyclopaedia Britannica 2005a. The Crusading Movement and the First Four Crusades. Encyclopaedia Britannica Premium Service. At www.britannica.com/eb/article?tocId=9110241.

Encyclopaedia Britannica 2005b. Cyrus II. Encyclopaedia Britannica Premium Service. At www.britannica.com/eb/article?tocId=9028433.

Encyclopaedia Britannica 2005c. Spain under the Catholic Monarchs. Encyclopaedia Britannica Premium Service. At www.britannica.com/eb/article?tocId=70387.

Evans, M. 1997. *Religious Liberty and International Law in Europe.* Cambridge: Cambridge University Press.

Figgis, J. 1922. *The Divine Right of Kings.* Cambridge: Cambridge University Press.

Freeman, M. 2002. *Human Rights: An Interdisciplinary Approach.* Cambridge: Polity.

Furnivall, J. 1948. *Colonial Policy and Practice.* Cambridge: Cambridge University Press.

Geary, P. 2002. *The Myth of Nations: The Medieval Origins of Europe.* Princeton: Princeton University Press.

Gellner, E. 1997. *Nationalism.* London: Weidenfeld and Nicolson.

Ghebali, V. 1998. Ethnicity in International Conflicts: Revisiting an Elusive Issue. Working Paper Series. Zurich: Centre for Security Studies and Conflict Research.

Glazer, N. and Moynihan, P. 1975. Introduction. In N. Glazer and P. Moynihan (eds), *Ethnicity: Theory and Experience.* Cambridge, Mass.: Harvard University Press.

Gobineau, A. 1915. *The Inequality of the Human Races,* trans. Adrian Collins. New York: G. P. Putnam's Sons.

Goldberg, D. 2001. *The Racial State.* Oxford: Blackwell.

Gong, G. 1984. *The Standard of Civilization in International Society.* Oxford: Clarendon Press.

Grieco, E. 2002. Defining 'Foreign Born' and 'Foreigner' in International Migration Statistics. *Migration Information Source,* Washington, D.C.: Migration Policy Institute.

Guardian, 17 March 2003. The Black Woman – with White Parents. At www.guardian.co.uk/g2/story/0,3604,915475,00.html.

Gutman, A. 1994. *Multiculturalism: Examining the Politics of Recognition.* Princeton: Princeton University Press.

Gutman, A. 2000. Should Public Policy be Class Conscious rather than Color Conscious? In S. Steinberg (ed.), *Race and Ethnicity in the United States: Issues and Debates.* Oxford: Blackwell.

Haddad, E. 2004. Between Sovereigns: The Refugee in International Society. Ph.D. thesis, London School of Economics.

Hailey, L. 1957. *An African Survey: A Study in Problems Arising in Africa South of the Sahara*. Revised edn, London: Oxford University Press.

Hannaford, I. 1996. *Race: The History of an Idea in the West*. Washington, DC: Woodrow Wilson Center Press.

Hayes, E. 1904. *Religious Persecution: A Study in Political Psychology*. London: Duckworth.

Helmreich, E. 1979. *The German Churches under Hitler: Background, Struggle and Epilogue*. Detroit: Wayne State University Press.

Hinsley, F. 1966. *Sovereignty*. London: Watts.

Hobbes, T. 1988. *Leviathan*. London: Everyman.

Hodgkin, T. 1957. *Nationalism in Colonial Africa*. New York: New York University Press.

Holy Bible, King James Version 2000. At www.bartleby.com/108/.

Horowitz, D. 1985. *Ethnic Groups in Conflict*. Berkeley: University of California Press.

Huntington, S. 1997. *The Clash of Civilizations and the Remaking of World Order*. New York: Touchstone.

Independent 29 October 2004. Schools Instructed to Provide Atheism Lessons alongside RE. At http://education.independent.co.uk/low_res/story.jsp?story=577134&host=16&dir=365.

Jackson, R. 2000. *The Global Covenant: Human Conduct in a World of States*. Oxford: Oxford University Press.

Jackson Preece, J. 1998a. Ethnic Cleansing as an Instrument of Nation-State Creation: Changing State Practices and Emerging Legal Norms. *Human Rights Quarterly*, 20 (4): 817–42.

Jackson Preece, J. 1998b. *National Minorities and the European Nation-States System*. Oxford: Clarendon Press.

Jackson Preece, J. 2003. Human Rights and Cultural Pluralism. In G. Lyons and J. Mayall (eds), *International Human Rights in the 21st Century: Protecting the Rights of Groups*. Oxford: Rowman and Littlefield.

Jarve, P. 2003. Language Battles in the Baltic States: 1989–2002. In F. Daftary and F. Grin (eds), *Nation-Building, Ethnicity and Language Politics in Transition Countries*. Budapest: Open Society Institute.

Jennings, I. 1956. *The Approach to Self-Government*. Cambridge: Cambridge University Press.

Kahlenberg, R. 2000. The Case for Class-Based Affirmation Action. In S. Steinberg (ed.), *Race and Ethnicity in the United States: Issues and Debates*. Oxford: Blackwell.

Kamen, H. 1967. *The Rise of Religious Toleration*. New York: McGraw-Hill.

Kedourie, E. 1960. *Nationalism*. London: Hutchinson University Library.

Klusmeyer, D. 1993. Aliens, Immigrants, and Citizens: The Politics of Inclusion in the Federal Republic of Germany. *Daedalus* 122 (3): 81–114.

Kohn, H. 1960. *The Idea of Nationalism*. New York: Macmillan.

Kymlicka, W. 1995. *Multicultural Citizenship*. Oxford: Oxford University Press.

Kymlicka, W. 2001. *Politics in the Vernacular*. Oxford: Oxford University Press.

Ladurie, E. 1979. *Montaillou: The Promised Land of Error*. New York: Vintage Books.

Laponce, J. 1960. *The Protection of Minorities*. Berkeley and Los Angeles: University of California Press.

League of Nations 1929. *Resolutions and Extracts of the Protection of Linguistic, Racial or Religious Minorities by the League of Nations*.

Lewis, B. 1982. *The Muslim Discovery of Europe*. New York: W. W. Norton.

Lindley, M. 1926. *The Acquisition and Government of Backward Territory in International Law*. London: Longmans, Green.

Lucas, C. 1922. *The Partition and Colonization of Africa*. Oxford: Clarendon Press.

Lugard, F. 1929. *The Dual Mandate of Africa*. 4th edn, London: William Blackwood.

Lyons, G. and Mayall, J. 2003. *International Human Rights in the 21st Century: Protecting the Rights of Groups*. Oxford: Rowman and Littlefield.

Macartney, C. 1934. *National States and National Minorities*. London: Oxford University Press.

Maqsood, R. 2003. *Teach Yourself Islam*. London: Hodder Headline.

Mastney, V. 1992. *The Helsinki Process and the Reintegration of Europe 1986–1991: Analysis and Documentation*. London: Pinter.

Mayall, J. 1990. *Nationalism and International Society*. Cambridge: Cambridge University Press.

Mazowar, M. 1998. *Dark Continent: Europe's Twentieth Century*. London: Penguin Press.

Mazrui, A. 1977. *Africa's International Relations*. London: Heinemann.

Mill, J. 1972. *Utilitarianism, On Liberty and Considerations on Representative Government*. London: J. M. Dent.

Minority Rights Group 1991. *Minorities and Human Rights Law*. London: Minority Rights Group International.

Moynihan, D. P. 1993. *Pandaemonium: Ethnicity in International Politics*. Oxford: Oxford University Press.

Namier, L. 1963. *Vanished Supremacies: Essays on European History, 1812–1918*. New York: Harper.

Nicholls, D. 1974. *Three Varieties of Pluralism*. New York: St Martin's Press.

Nicolson, H. 1945. *Peacemaking 1919*. London: Constable.

Oakley, F. 1988. *The Medieval Experience*. Toronto: University of Toronto Press.

Oldham, J. 1924. *Christianity and the Race Problem*. London: Student Christian Movement.

Organization for Security and Cooperation in Europe 1999. Report on Laws Affecting the Structuring of Religious Communities. At www.osce.org/documents/odihr/1999/09/1502_en.html.

Oxford English Dictionary (OED) 1989. 2nd edn, Oxford: Oxford University Press.

Pagden, A. 2001. *Peoples and Empires: A Short History of European Migration, Exploration, and Conquest from Greece to the Present*. New York: Modern Library.

Perham, M. 1967. *Colonial Sequence, 1930 to 1949*. London: Methuen.

Poulton, H. 1991. *Balkans: Minorities and States in Conflict*. London: Minority Rights Group.

Powell, E. 1968. 'Rivers of Blood' speech. At www.hippy.freeserve.co.uk/rofblood.htm.

Prucha, F. 1997. *American Indian Treaties: The History of a Political Anomaly*. Berkeley: University of California Press.

Rawls, J. 1993. *Political Liberalism*. New York: Columbia University Press.

Raz, J. 1986. *The Morality of Freedom*. Oxford: Clarendon Press.

Reynolds, S. 1990. *Kingdoms and Communities in Western Europe 900–1300*. Oxford: Clarendon Press.

Schulze, H. 1998. *States, Nations and Nationalism*. Oxford: Blackwell.

Seton-Watson, H. 1977. *Nations and States: An Inquiry into the Origins of Nations and the Politics of Nationalism*. London: Methuen.

Shafer, B. 1955. *Nationalism: Myth and Reality*. New York: Harcourt, Brace and World.

Shklar, J. 1986. *Legalism*. Cambridge, Mass.: Harvard University Press.

Showalter, R. 1996. All the Clans, All the Peoples. *International Journal of Frontier Missions*, 13 (1): 1–3.

Sieghart, P. 1986. *The Lawful Rights of Mankind*. Oxford: Oxford University Press.

SikhSpectrum.com 2002. A Celebrated Sikh Officer and Gentleman. Issue no. 4, September 2002. At www.sikhspectrum.com/092002/baltej.htm.

Silber, L. and Little, A. 1996. *The Death of Yugoslavia*. 2nd edn, London: Penguin Books.

Smith, A. 1986. *The Ethnic Origins of Nations*. Oxford: Blackwell.

Snyder, J. 2000. *From Voting to Violence, Democratization and Nationalist Conflict*. New York: W. W. Norton.

Sohn, L. 1995. The Human Rights Movement: From Roosevelt's Four Freedoms to the Interdependence of Peace, Development and Human

Rights. The Edward A. Smith Visiting Lecture, Cambridge, Mass.: Harvard Law School Human Rights Programme. At www.law.harvard.edu/programs/hrp/Publications/sohn.html#TOC.

Southern, R. 1993. *The Making of the Middle Ages*. London: Pimlico.

Spencer, H. 1969. Man versus the State. In W. Ebenstein, *Great Political Thinkers*. New York: Holt, Rinehart and Winston.

Steinberg, S. 2000. Occupational Apartheid and the Origins of Affirmative Action. In S. Steinberg (ed.), *Race and Ethnicity in the United States: Issues and Debates*. Oxford: Blackwell.

Stephen Lawrence Inquiry 1999. *Report of an Inquiry by Sir William MacPherson of Cluny*. London: Stationery Office.

Story, J. 1833. *Commentaries on the Constitution of the United States*. Cambridge, Mass.: Brown, Shattuck. At www.constitution.org/js/js_000.htm.

Thornberry, P. 1991. *International Law and the Rights of Minorities*. Oxford: Clarendon Press.

Trevelyan, G. 1965. *The English Revolution: 1688–89*, London: Oxford University Press.

United Kingdom 1819. *Parliamentary Debates*. Vol. 40: cols. 433–8.

United Nations 1949. *Definition and Classification of Minorities*. E/CN.4/SUB.2/83.

United Nations 1981. *Sandra Lovelace v. Canada*, Communication No. R.6/24, UN Doc. Supp. No. 40 (A/36/40) at 166 (1981).

United Nations 2001. *Civil and Political Rights Including Religious Intolerance*. E/CN.4/2001/63.

United States Department of State 2003a. Croatia. *Annual Report on International Religious Freedom*. At www.state.gov/g/drl/rls/irf/2003/24350.htm.

United States Department of State 2003b. Israel and the Occupied Territories. *Annual Report on International Religious Freedom*. At www.state.gov/g/drl/rls/irf/2003/24453.htm.

United States Department of State 2003c. Serbia and Montenegro. *Annual Report on International Religious Freedom*. At www.state.gov/g/drl/rls/irf/2003/27248.htm.

United States Department of State 2003d. Saudi Arabia. *Annual Report on International Religious Freedom*. At www.state.gov/g/drl/rls/irf/2003/24461.htm.

Van der Vyver, J. and J. Witte (eds). 1996. *Religious Human Rights in Global Perspective: Legal Perspectives*. The Hague: Martinus Nijhoff.

Vincent R. 1986. *Human Rights and International Relations*. Cambridge: Cambridge University Press.

Vincent, R. 1992. Racial Equality. In H. Bull and A. Watson (eds), *The Expansion of International Society*. Oxford: Oxford University Press.

Watson, A. 1992. *The Evolution of International Society*. London: Routledge.

Wertheimer, J. 1987. *Unwelcome Strangers: East European Jews in Imperial Germany.* New York: Oxford University Press.

Wight, M. 1952. *British Colonial Constitutions 1947.* Oxford: Clarendon Press.

Wight, M. 1977. *Systems of States.* Leicester: Leicester University Press.

Wuthnow, R. 1998. *Encyclopedia of Politics and Religion.* Washington, DC: Congressional Quarterly.

Index